Configuring IPCop Firewalls
Closing Borders with Open Source

How to set up, configure, and manage your Linux
firewall, web proxy, DHCP, DNS, time server, and VPN
with this powerful Open Source solution

Barrie Dempster

James Eaton-Lee

BIRMINGHAM - MUMBAI

Configuring IPCop Firewalls

Closing Borders with Open Source

First published: September 2006

Production Reference: 1160906

Published by Packt Publishing Ltd.
32 Lincoln Road
Olton
Birmingham, B27 6PA, UK.

ISBN 1-904811-36-1

www.packtpub.com

Cover Image by www.visionwt.com

Credits

Authors

Barrie Dempster

James Eaton-Lee

Reviewers

Kyle Hutson

Lawrence Bean

Development Editor

Louay Fatoohi

Assistant Development Editor

Nikhil Bangera

Technical Editor

Saurabh Singh

Editorial Manager

Dipali Chittar

Indexer

Mithil Kulkarni

Proofreader

Chris Smith

Layouts and Illustrations

Shantanu Zagade

Cover Designer

Shantanu Zagade

About the Authors

Barrie Dempster is currently employed as a Senior Security Consultant for NGS Software Ltd, a world-renowned security consultancy well known for its focus in enterprise-level application vulnerability research and database security. He has a background in Infrastructure and Information Security in a number of specialized environments such as financial services institutions, telecommunications companies, call centers, and other organizations across multiple continents. Barrie has experience in the integration of network infrastructure and telecommunications systems requiring high caliber secure design, testing, and management. He has been involved in a variety of projects from the design and implementation of Internet banking systems to large-scale conferencing and telephony infrastructure, as well as penetration testing and other security assessments of business-critical infrastructure.

James Eaton-Lee works as a Consultant specializing in Infrastructure Security; he has worked with clients ranging from small businesses with a handful of employees to multinational banks. He has a varied background, including experience working with IT in ISPs, manufacturing firms, and call centers. James has been involved in the integration of a range of systems, from analog and VoIP telephony to NT and AD domains in mission-critical environments with thousands of hosts, as well as UNIX & Linux servers in a variety of roles. James is a strong advocate of the use of appropriate technology, and the need to make technology more approachable and flexible for businesses of all sizes, but especially in the SME marketplace in which technology is often forgotten and avoided. James has been a strong believer in the relevancy and merit of Open Source and Free Software for a number of years and — wherever appropriate — uses it for himself and his clients, integrating it fluidly with other technologies.

About the Reviewers

Kyle Hutson is a Networking Consultant for Network Resource Group, Inc. in Manhattan, Kansas, where he designs, implements, and fixes computers and networks for small businesses. His networking career spans 15 years, and has included UNIX, Linux, Novell, Macintosh, and Windows networks. Kyle stumbled upon IPCop while looking for a replacement for a broken firewall appliance. Since then, he has installed it for several clients. He remains active on the IPCop-user mailing list.

Lawrence Bean fell out of Computer Science and into Music Education in his sophomore year of college. He graduated from the University of Maine with a Bachelor's in Music Education in 1986 and had a ten year career as a Choral Music Educator in the Kennebunk, Maine school system. His large non-audition groups won silver at the Events America Choral Festival and his select group was featured on Good Morning America and in Yankee Magazine for its annual performances of traditional Christmas carols at the highly acclaimed Kennebunkport Christmas Prelude. Throughout his music tenure he maintained his involvement in computers as the unofficial "computer dude" for Kennebunk Middle School, as well as integrating the use of computer applications throughout all aspects of the music education program. He fell back into Computer Science with the offer of a position as Technology Coordinator at SU#47 in greater Bath, Maine. For the last ten years he has taught teachers how to teach using technology in the classroom as well as creating and managing all aspects of the technology program from hardware repair to network design to database management. He completed his Masters in Computer Science at the University of Southern Maine in 2006.

Throughout his technology tenure he has maintained his involvement in music by bringing the Maine All-State Auditions into the 21st century with on-line applications, judging, and results processing. Outside of work and school, his 16-year career with The Management barbershop quartet brought two albums, a district championship, three trips to the international competition stage, Barbershopper of the Year for the Northeastern District, and the national MENC/SPEBSQSA Educator of the Year award. In his spare time he presents workshops and seminars on technology integration in education, has guest-directed more than half the district music festivals in Maine, created an "open-source" student information system for use by small Maine schools, and recently had an original 8-part a capella composition premiered by the University of Maine Singers. Lawrence lives with his very patient wife Betsy in Saco, Maine.

Table of Contents

Preface

IPCop is a Linux-based, stateful firewall distribution that sits in between your Internet connection and your network and directs traffic using a set of rules framed by you. It provides most of the features that you would expect a modern firewall to have, and what is most important is that it sets this all up for you in a highly automated and simplified way.

This book is an easy-to-read guide to using IPCop in a variety of different roles within the network. The book is written in a very friendly style that makes this complex topic easy and a joy to read. It first covers basic IPCop concepts, then moves to introduce basic IPCop configurations, before covering advanced uses of IPCop. This book is for both experienced and new IPCop users.

What This Book Covers

Chapter 1 briefly introduces some firewall and networking concepts. The chapter introduces the roles of several common networking devices and explains how firewalls fit into this.

Chapter 2 introduces the IPCop package itself, discussing how IPCop's red/orange/ blue/green interfaces fit into a network topology. It then covers the configuration of IPCop in other common roles, such as those of a web proxy, DHCP, DNS, time, and VPN server.

Chapter 3 covers three sample scenarios where we learn how to deploy IPCop, and how IPCop interfaces connect to each other and to the network as a whole.

Chapter 4 covers installing IPCop. It outlines the system configuration required to run IPCop, and explains the configuration required to get IPCop up and running.

Chapter 5 explains how to employ the various tools IPCop provides us with to administer, operate, troubleshoot, and monitor our IPCop firewall.

Chapter 6 starts off with explaining the need for an IDS in our system and then goes on to explain how to use the SNORT IDS with IPCop.

Chapter 7 introduces the VPN concept and explains how to set up an IPSec VPN configuration for a system. Special focus is laid on configuring the blue zone—a secured wireless network augmenting the security of a wireless segment, even one already using WEP or WPA.

Chapter 8 demonstrates how to manage bandwidth using IPCop making use of traffic-shaping techniques and cache management. The chapter also covers the configuration of the Squid web proxy and caching system.

Chapter 9 focuses on the vast range of addons available to configure IPCop to suit our needs. We see how to install addons and then learn more about common addons like SquidGuard, Enhanced Filtering, Blue Access, LogSend, and CopFilter.

Chapter 10 covers IPCop security risks, patch management, and some security and auditing tools and tests.

Chapter 11 outlines the support IPCop users have in the form of mailing lists and IRC.

What You Need for This Book

IPCop runs on a dedicated box, and it *completely takes over the hard drive*, so don't use a drive with anything valuable on it. It will run on old or "obsolete" hardware, such as a 386 processor, 32Mb of RAM, and 300Mb hard disk. But if you plan on using some of IPCop's features, such as the caching web proxy, or Intrusion Detection Logging, you are going to need more RAM, more disk space, and a faster processor.

At least one Network Interface Card NIC is *required* for the Green Interface. If you will be connecting to the Internet via a cable modem, you will need two NICs.

Once installed you don't need to have a monitor or keyboard attached to the IPCop box, as it runs as a *headless* server, and is administered over the network with a web browser.

Conventions

In this book, you will find a number of styles of text that distinguish between different kinds of information. Here are some examples of these styles, and an explanation of their meaning.

There are three styles for code. Code words in text are shown as follows: " In Windows, the `ipconfig` command also allows the user to release and renew DHCP information."

A block of code will be set as follows:

```
james@horus: ~ $ sudo nmap 10.10.2.32 -T Insane -O

Starting nmap 3.81 ( http://www.insecure.org/nmap/ ) at 2006-05-02
21:36 BST
Interesting ports on 10.10.2.32:
(The 1662 ports scanned but not shown below are in state: closed)
PORT    STATE SERVICE
22/tcp open  ssh
MAC Address: 00:30:AB:19:23:A9 (Delta Networks)
Device type: general purpose
Running: Linux 2.4.X|2.5.X|2.6.X
OS details: Linux 2.4.18 - 2.6.7
Uptime 0.034 days (since Tue May  2 20:47:15 2006)

Nmap finished: 1 IP address (1 host up) scanned in 8.364 seconds
```

Any command-line input and output is written as follows:

```
# mv /addons /addons.bak
# tar xzvf /addons-2.3-CLI-b2.tar.gz -C /
# cd /addons
# ./addoncfg -u
# ./addoncfg -i
```

New terms and **important words** are introduced in a bold-type font. Words that you see on the screen, in menus or dialog boxes for example, appear in our text like this: "We then go back to the addons page, click the **Browse** button, browse to the file we just downloaded, click **Upload**, and the addon is installed on the server."

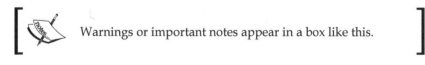

Warnings or important notes appear in a box like this.

Tips and tricks appear like this.

Reader Feedback

Feedback from our readers is always welcome. Let us know what you think about this book, what you liked or may have disliked. Reader feedback is important for us to develop titles that you really get the most out of.

To send us general feedback, simply drop an email to feedback@packtpub.com, making sure to mention the book title in the subject of your message.

If there is a book that you need and would like to see us publish, please send us a note in the **SUGGEST A TITLE** form on www.packtpub.com or email suggest@packtpub.com.

If there is a topic that you have expertise in and you are interested in either writing or contributing to a book, see our author guide on www.packtpub.com/authors.

Customer Support

Now that you are the proud owner of a Packt book, we have a number of things to help you to get the most from your purchase.

Downloading the Example Code for the Book

Visit http://www.packtpub.com/support, and select this book from the list of titles to download any example code or extra resources for this book. The files available for download will then be displayed.

The downloadable files contain instructions on how to use them.

Errata

Although we have taken every care to ensure the accuracy of our contents, mistakes do happen. If you find a mistake in one of our books—maybe a mistake in text or code—we would be grateful if you would report this to us. By doing this you can save other readers from frustration, and help to improve subsequent versions of this book. If you find any errata, report them by visiting http://www.packtpub.com/support, selecting your book, clicking on the **Submit Errata** link, and entering the details of your errata. Once your errata have been verified, your submission will be accepted and the errata added to the list of existing errata. The existing errata can be viewed by selecting your title from http://www.packtpub.com/support.

Questions

You can contact us at questions@packtpub.com if you are having a problem with some aspect of the book, and we will do our best to address it.

1
Introduction to Firewalls

In this chapter, we will introduce some firewalling and networking concepts in enough detail to provide a refresher to those who've encountered them already, but in as minimal a fashion as possible, since understanding networking concepts is not the focus of this book. We feel that some of these concepts are important, and that a broader picture of how these technologies are used and where they come from serves to better our understanding of the way in which IT works—however, for the reader who is challenged for time, we have tried, wherever possible, to provide *italicized* summaries of the knowledge that we feel is important to have about these concepts.

Don't worry if you don't understand all of the concepts we discuss—equally, readers more comfortable with networking concepts should be able to skip ahead. IPCop makes explicit understanding of many of these concepts irrelevant, as it attempts to make administration simple and automated wherever possible. However, if you do feel inclined to learn about these topics in more depth, the introduction given here and some of the URLs and links to other resources that we provide should hopefully be of use. Understanding networking, routing, and how some common protocols work, although not a requirement, will also help you immeasurably if you intend to keep working with systems such as IPCop on a regular basis.

An Introduction to (TCP/IP) Networking

During the early 1970s, as data networks became more common, the number of different ways in which to build them increased exponentially. To a number of people, the concept of *internetworking (IBM TCP/IP Tutorial and Technical Overview, Martin W. Murhammer, Orcun Atakan, Stefan Bretz, Larry R. Pugh, Kazunari Suzuki, David H. Wood, October 1998, pp3)*, or *connecting multiple networks to each other*, became extremely important as connecting together disparate and contrasting networks built around different sets of technology started causing pain.

A protocol, within the context of IT and Computer Science, is generally speaking a common format in which computers interchange data for a certain purpose. In networking, a protocol is best compared to a language — the networking situation in the 1970s was one in which there were many different languages and very few interpreters readily available to translate for people.

The resulting research, and most importantly that carried out and funded by the American Department of Defense's *Defense Advanced Research Projects Agency* (http://www.darpa.mil), gave birth not only to a range of network *protocols* designed for interoperability (that is to say, in order to allow easy, platform-neutral communications between a range of devices), but a network, **ARPANet**, set up for this express purpose. The best comparison for this within language is the development of the language *Esperanto* — although the proliferation of this *international* language has been fairly minimal, computers have the advantage of not taking years to learn a particular protocol!

This ARPANet was first experimented with using TCP/IP in 1976, and in January of 1983, its use was mandated for all computers participating in the network. By the late 1970s, many organizations besides the military were granted access to the ARPANet as well, such as NASA, the **National Science Foundation** (**NSF**), and eventually universities and other academic entities.

After the military broke away from the ARPANet to form its own, separate network for military use (**MILNET**), the network became the responsibility of the NSF, which came to create its own high-speed backbone, called **NSFNet**, for the facilitation of internetworking.

When the Acceptable Usage Policy for NSFNet began to permit non-academic traffic, the NSFNet began, in combination with other (commercial and private) networks (such as those operated via CIX), to form the entity we now know as the Internet. By the NSF's exit from the management of the Internet and the shutdown of the NSFNet in April 1995, the Internet was populated by an ever-growing population of commercial, academic, and private users.

The standards upon which the Internet is based have become the staple of modern networking, and nowadays when anyone says 'networking' they tend to be referring to something built with (and around) **TCP/IP**, the set of layered protocols originally developed for use on ARPANet, along with other standards upon which TCP/IP is implemented, such as **802.3** or **Ethernet,** which defines how one of the most popular standards over which TCP/IP runs across in network segments works.

These layered protocols, apart from being interesting to us for historical and anecdotal reasons, have several important implications for us. The most notable implication is that any device built around them is entirely interoperable with any other device. The consequence of this, then, is that we can buy networking components built by any vendor—our Dell laptop running Microsoft Windows can freely communicate, via TCP/IP, over an Ethernet network using a Linksys switch, plugged into a Cisco Router, and view a web page hosted on an IBM server running AIX, also talking TCP/IP.

More standardized protocols, running on top of TCP/IP, such as HTTP, actually carry the information itself, and thanks to the layering of these protocols, we can have a vast and disparate set of networks connected that appear transparent to devices such as web browsers and web servers, that speak protocols such as HTTP. Between our Dell laptop and our IBM server, we may have a dial-up connection, a frame relay network segment, a portion of the internet backbone, and a wireless network link—none of which concern TCP/IP or HTTP, which sit 'above' these layers of the network, and travel freely above them. If only a coach load of children on a school tour could use air travel, ferries, cycle paths, and cable cars, all without stepping from their vehicle or being aware of the changing transport medium beneath them! Layered communication of the type that TCP/IP is capable of in this sense is incredibly powerful and really allows our communications infrastructure to scale.

The Purpose of Firewalls

This network and the research underpinning it, originally funded based on the utility for military purposes in one country, has far surpassed its original aims, and through international research and uptake, spawned a phenomenon that is shaping (and will shape) generations to come. Networking is now a core activity not just to governments and research organizations, but also to companies small and large, and even home users. Further developments such as the inception of wireless technology have served to make this technology even more accessible (and relevant) to people at home, on the go, and in the imminent future, virtually anywhere on the surface of the planet!

Many of these networking protocols were originally designed in an environment in which the word '*hacker*' had not yet come to have the (negative) meaning that it nowadays has, and implemented upon a network in which there was a culture of mutual trust and respect. **IPv4**, the foundation of all communications via the Internet (and the majority of private networks) and **SMTP** (the protocol used to send electronic mail and relay it from to server to server) are two prime examples of this. Neither protocol, in its initial incarnation, was designed with features designed to maintain the three qualities that nowadays are synonymous with effective communication, **Confidentiality**, **Integrity**, and **Availability** (called the **CIA triad**). The CIA triad is often defined as the aim of information security—`http://en.wikipedia.org/wiki/CIA_triad`. *Spam* and *Denial of Service attacks* are just two examples of (malicious) exploitations of some of the weaknesses in these two protocols.

As networking technologies grew and were adopted by governments and large organizations that relied upon them, the need for these three qualities increased, and network firewalls became a necessity. In short, the need for *network security* sprung into existence. The Internet has come a long way too from its humble beginnings. As the barrier for entry has decreased, and knowledge of the technologies underpinning it has become more accessible, it has become a decreasingly friendly place.

With growing reliance on the Internet for communications, firewalls have, at time of writing, become almost universally deployed as a primary line of defense against unauthorized network activity, automated attacks, and inside abuse. They are deployed everywhere, and the term 'firewall' is used in this context to refer to anything from a software stack built into commonly used operating systems (such as the *Windows firewall* built into Service Pack 2 of Microsoft's Windows Operating System (`http://www.microsoft.com/windowsxp/using/security/internet/sp2_wfintro.mspx`)) protecting only the computer it is running on, to devices costing significant sums of money deployed in banks, datacenters, and government facilities (such as Cisco's PIX line of firewall products (`http://www.cisco.com/en/US/products/hw/vpndevc/ps2030/`)). Such high-end devices may govern and restrict network traffic between hundreds of thousands of individual computers.

Given this increase in the use of the term 'firewall', and with so many qualifiers added to the word to distinguish between different types of firewall (such as the terms stateful, proxy, application, packet filter, hardware, software, circuit-level, and many more), it becomes very difficult to know what someone means when they tell you that their network "has a firewall". Our exploration of IPCop, therefore, must begin with an exploration of what a firewall actually is, and armed with this knowledge, we can then relate IPCop to this knowledge and understand what function it is that IPCop can fulfill for us.

In order to improve our network security, we need to first identify the problems we need to solve, and determine whether this firewall is the solution to them. Implementing a firewall for the sake of satisfying the buzzword requirement is a common mistake in security design.

The term firewall refers, generally, to a collection of technologies and devices all designed to do one thing—stop unauthorized network activity. A firewall acts as a choke point between more than one network (or network segment), and uses a (hopefully) strictly defined set of rules in order to allow, or disallow, certain types of traffic to traverse to the other side of the firewall. Most importantly, it is a security boundary between two or more networks.

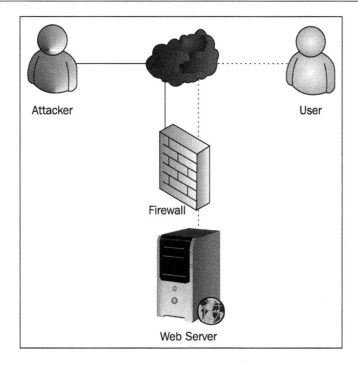

In the diagram above, a web server connected to the Internet is protected by a firewall, which sits in between it and the Internet, filtering all incoming and outgoing traffic. In this scenario, illegitimate traffic from the attacker is blocked by the firewall. This could be for any number of reasons, such as the service the attacker has attempted to connect is blocked by the firewall from the Internet, because the attacker's network address is blacklisted, or because the type of traffic the attacker is sending is recognized by the firewall as being part of a Denial of Service attack.

In this scenario, the network that the web server sits on (which in a scenario such as this would probably contain multiple web servers) is segmented from the Internet by the firewall, effectively implementing a security policy dictating *what* can go from one network (or collection of networks) to the other. If our firewall disallowed the attacker from connecting to a file-sharing port on the web server, for instance, while the 'user' was free to access the web server on port 80, the other servers behind the firewall might be allowed access to the file sharing ports in order to synchronize content or make backups.

Layered protocols are generally explained using the **Open System Interconnection (OSI)** layers. Knowledge of this is extremely useful to anyone working in networking or with firewalls in particular, as so many of the concepts pertaining to it require knowledge of the way in which this layering works.

The OSI layers divide traffic and data into seven layers each of which in theory falls into a protocol. Although excellent in theory, networking and IT applications do not always strictly adhere to the OSI Layers, and it is worth considering them to be guidelines rather than a strict framework. That said, they are extremely useful for visualizing connectivity, and in general the vision of layers, each utilizing hardware and software designed by different vendors, each interoperating with the layers above and below is not unrealistic.

The OSI Model

The OSI model is shown in the following figure:

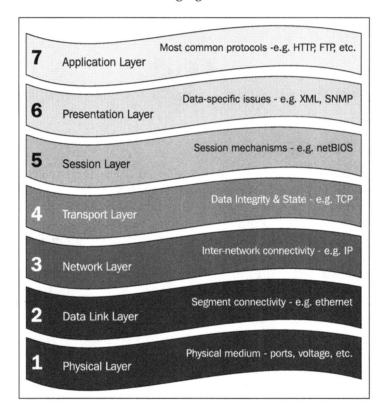

Layer 1: The Physical Layer

The physical layer encompasses the physical medium on which a network is built. Specifications that operate within the physical layer include physical interfaces such as ports, voltages, pin specifications, cable design, and materials. A **network hub** is a layer-one device.

Layer 2: The Data Link Layer

The data link layer provides connectivity between hosts on the same network segment. **MAC** addresses are used at the physical layer to distinguish between different physical network adapters and allow them to communicate. **Ethernet** is a layer-two standard.

Layer 3: The Network Layer

The network layer provides connectivity between hosts on different networks, and it is at this layer that routing occurs. **Internet Protocol** (**IP**) and **Address Resolution Protocol** (**ARP**) exist at this layer. ARP serves an important purpose, as it intermediates between layer two and layer three by ascertaining the layer-two (MAC) address for a given layer-three (IP) address.

Layer 4: The Transport Layer

The transport layer, generally, acts as the layer that ensures data integrity. **TCP**, the protocol most frequently used at this layer, is a **stateful** protocol that, by maintaining connections with a remote host, can retransmit data that does not reach the destination. **UDP**, another (slightly less common) protocol also operates at this layer, but is not stateful—each message it sends is not part of a 'connection' as such, and is treated as entirely separate to a reply (if one is required) or any messages previously passed between two hosts.

IP, TCP/IP, UDP, and other Layer four protocols

As we can see from the examination of the OSI Layers, TCP is a protocol running on top of IP, forming the abbreviation TCP/IP. Unfortunately, when people use the term TCP/IP, this specific pair of protocols is not always what they mean—the 'TCP/IP Protocol Suite' is quite frequently defined to be IP, TCP, and other protocols such as UDP and ICMP that are used along with it. This is a distinction that it is worth being aware of, and which is particularly common amongst IT professionals, and in the documentation for operating systems such as Microsoft's Windows.

Layer 5: The Session Layer

The upper three layers in the OSI model are no longer concerned with (inter-) networking issues as such, and have more to do with the practicalities of software and applications that use connectivity. The session layer is where mechanisms for setting up sessions live, such as the **NetBIOS** protocol.

Layer 6: The Presentation Layer

The presentation layer handles data-specific issues such as encoding, compression, and encryption. **SNMP** and **XML** are standards often used, which exist at this layer.

Layer 7: The Application Layer

The application layer is the layer at which common protocols used for communication live, such as **HTTP**, **FTP**, and **SMTP**.

Generally, Layers three and four, are the ones most commonly dealt with by firewalls, with a small (but increasing) number, generally referred to as 'proxy firewalls' or 'application-layer firewalls' sitting at layers above this (and being aware of protocols like HTTP, DNS, RCP, and NetBIOS). It is worth noting that many firewalls (incorrectly) classify all layers above layer three as *application layers*.

For our purposes, a thorough understanding (and explanation) of OSI layers and some of the more conceptual and technical aspects of networking are unnecessary — although we have tried to provide some outline of these, this is more for familiarity and in order to give you some idea as to what you may want to learn in future.

For our purposes a knowledge that layering exists is sufficient. If you feel the need (or are otherwise so inclined) to learn more about these topics, some of the URLs given in this chapter serve as good starting points for this. You don't necessarily have to understand, agree with, or like the OSI layers in order to work with firewalls (in fact, many TCP/IP stacks do not strictly adhere to segment handling of traffic based on them), but knowing that they exist and understanding approximately what they're designed to do and how the technologies built around them interact is important to anyone serious about understanding firewalls or networking or for anyone who regularly works with these technologies.

In many instances, Wikipedia (`http://www.wikipedia.org`) serves as a good starting reference for technical concepts where the (ostensibly well versed in IT) audience of wikipedia really shine at providing comprehensive coverage of topics! The wikipedia OSI Layer page is well referenced and has technically accurate content. This can be found at `http://en.wikipedia.org/wiki/OSI_seven-layer_model`.

Another excellent online resource for information on all things on TCP/IP is `http://tcpipguide.com/`.

The IBM "TCP/IP Tutorial and Technical Overview" referenced earlier in this chapter, by Martin W. Murhammer, Orcun Atakan, Stefan Bretz, Larry R. Pugh, Kazunari Suzuki, and David H. Wood, is another good (and free) guide to the world of TCP/IP networking. Although slightly out of date (the last iteration was published in October 1998), many of the standards surrounding TCP/IP have not changed in over 20 years, so the date should not put you off too much. This guide, and many others pertaining to open standards and IBM products can be found at the excellent 'IBM Redbooks' site at `http://www.redbooks.ibm.com/`.

For a published introduction to TCP/IP, the three "TCP/IP Illustrated" books by Richard W. Stevens are generally considered to be the authoritative source on the topic. The ISBN number for the complete set is 0-201-77631-6, and it can be found at any good major bookstore or online book retailer.

How Networks are Structured

Whether you know it or not, the chances are that any network that you use is build on top of IP, Internet Protocol. IP and the protocols that are built on top of it (such as TCP, UDP, and ICMP, all of which use IP datagrams) are the foundation of almost every network presently deployed. The components that such networks are built out of are interoperable, and for these reasons their roles are well defined and well understood. We will, briefly, talk about these devices and—particularly—how they interconnect with firewalls.

Ethernet, as the underlying technology on top of which most of these protocols are generally layered, forms the basis of these devices. As such network devices, peripherals, and appliances are often referred to as **LAN**, Ethernet, or TCP/IP equipment (or more commonly, just "**Network**" equipment). There are other networking standards in use, two of them being **Token Ring** and **SNA** networks that have fairly specific uses. Many of theses standards including the two mentioned above, are generally considered outdated. It is commonly the case that in scenarios in which they are still deployed for legacy reasons, such networks, are hallmarked for replacement or are effectively change-frozen.

As a point of interest, Token Ring and SNA are often deployed in larger organizations, the latter almost unilaterally in communication with a mainframe such as IBM zSeries. Other specialized IT environments, such as clustering, have specific networking requirements that draw them towards other forms of networking also.

Here, however, we shall consider the following (Ethernet/IP) network devices:

- Servers and clients (microcomputers)
- Switches and Hubs
- Routers
- Combined Devices

Servers and Clients

The server/client relationship is the cornerstone of the TCP/IP protocol and it is necessary to have some understanding of it in order to be able to effectively administer, implement, and think about it. Put very simply, a client is any device that initiates a connection (i.e. commences sending data) to another computer, and a server is any device that listens for such a connection in order to allow others to connect to it.

Within the context of TCP/IP, all devices on a network are servers and clients, irrespective of whether or not they are specifically assigned the role of server (such as a corporate mail server) or client (such as a desktop computer). This is for two reasons: firstly, many higher-level protocols initiate connections back to clients from the server itself; secondly, a TCP/IP connection actually involves data being sent to listening ports in both connections — initially from the client to the server in order to commence the transaction, connecting (generally) to a well-known port on the server in order to access a specific service (such as port 80 for HTTP, port 25 for SMTP, or port 21 for FTP) with traffic coming from a (generally) random ephemeral (i.e. greater than 1024) port on the client.

Once this data arrives, the server sends data to the client (and in this connection, the server is a client!) from the service port and to the (random) port on the client that was used as the source port for the initial connection. Traffic from the service port on the server to the client is used in order for the server to reply to the client. Data flowing in both directions, from client to server and server to client, constitutes a 'whole' TCP/IP connection. This particular distinction becomes important later on when we discuss traffic filtering.

Within the context of a network, a server is a device that provides a fixed service to hosts on that network. Generally this involves some form of centraliszed resource; although a 'firewall' may be described as a server it doesn't necessarily have to accept connections to itself (but rather facilitates connections to other locations and/or servers).

A server may serve files, email, or web pages, provide network configuration information via DHCP, provide translation between Domain Names and Host Names and IP addresses acting as a DNS server, or even provide other, more complex services, which facilitate single sign on or provide security services (such as Kerberos servers, radius servers, intrusion detection systems, etc.). For the purposes of this book, we will — generally — consider a server to be a *device that provides services and data to other computers and devices on a network.*

Clients are generally used directly by users and will be situated on desks and have monitors and input devices plugged into them, or are laptops (servers frequently either share such peripherals or don't have them at all). They are directly used to access resources and information that is sometimes stored elsewhere (such as web pages or files from a file server) or locally (such as documents stored on a local My Documents folder). For the purposes of this book, we will, generally, consider a client to be a *device that a user uses to access services on other computers (and access data stored on them) on a network or on the Internet.*

 For more information on the client/server relationship, see http://en.wikipedia.org/wiki/Client-server.

Switches and Hubs

The hub is a networking device that allows multiple clients to be plugged into the network segment, within the context of which they can communicate with each other. A hub is, logically, very simple, and essentially acts as a logical connector for all devices attached to the device, allowing traffic to freely flow from port to port, such that in a four-port device, if the client attached to port 1 sends data to the client attached to port 4, the hub (unaware of the concept of 'clients') simply allows this traffic to flow to all ports on this device — clients 2 and 3 ignore the traffic not destined for them.

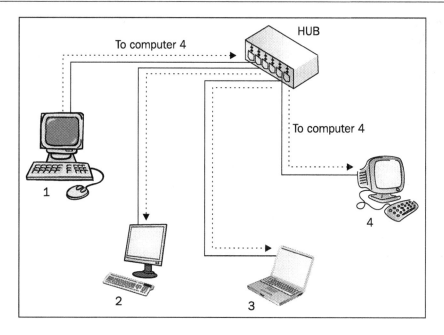

Switches address several shortcomings of hubs and are typically deployed in preference to them. Increasingly, in addition, hubs are becoming a relic of a previous age, and are becoming very hard to purchase at retail outlets and online.

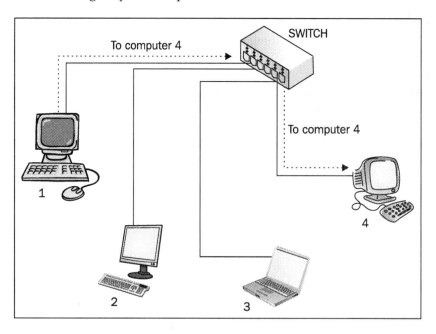

Switches work by keeping a table in memory correlating ports with MAC addresses, such that the switch knows which computers are plugged into which port. Some switches, which can be 'stacked', apply this to the entire network segment, although in a network in which unmanaged or un-stacked switches were simply connected to each other by crossover cabling, a given switch would simply see a large number of MAC addresses on a particular port.

Since traffic on local segments (even traffic being routed through that segment and destined for another network) is passed from host to host (router to router, router to client, client to server, etc.) directly by MAC address, the switch can make a decision based on the ports it has, as to for which port a particular datagram is intended. As processing is required, switches have historically been more expensive than hubs, as the electronics required to perform such processing costs more than the 'stupid' components inside a hub.

In terms of their advantages, switches are faster, since any two ports may use a large quantity of bandwidth without affecting the bandwidth available to other ports on the device. On an unswitched network, if clients 1 and 4 are generating traffic at 90% of the available bandwidth, there is only 10% of the bandwidth (or, practically, less, when dealing with overhead imposed by IP) available for the rest of the network. On a switched network, each port, logically, has a significantly increased bandwidth limit, typically up to the limit of the hardware of the switch.

It is worth noting that many switches will have an overall bandwidth limit for traffic through all ports, and most medium to higher-end switches have an 'uplink' port, which in addition to providing MDI-X ability (the ability to sense whether a crossover link is required, and if so, perform the necessary modification in the switch, so a normal 'patch' cable can be used for a switch-to-switch connection) is also a higher bandwidth port (gigabit on a 100 megabit switch), or is a GBIC interface enabling a modular uplink.

Switches are also inherently slightly more secure as it is harder for any device to arbitrarily listen to network traffic, which may contain private data or authentication information such as passwords. Switches understand which clients are plugged into which socket on the switch, and will under normal circumstances move data from one port to another without passing unrelated traffic to computers not acting as the destination.

This is not, however, an absolute security measure, and may be circumvented using a technique known as ARP Spoofing or ARP Poisoning (`http://www.node99.org/projects/arpspoof/`). **ARP Spoofing** is a very well-known technique, with several tools existing for multiple platforms in order to allow people to perform it. On a local segment, ARP spoofing allows any user with administrator or system-level access to a PC (administrator credentials, a spare network socket into which to plug a laptop, or just a computer configured to boot from CD or floppy disk) to intercept any and all traffic sent by other computers on the same segment, and redirect it transparently to the Internet (or another destination) without any visible disruption to the user. Once this layer-two protocol is compromised, every other protocol at every other layer (with the exception of strong cryptographic protocols involving handshakes that are hard to attack, or using certificates) must be considered to be compromised as well.

Modern switches often have many forms of advanced functionality. Traditional switches, although more intelligent than hubs, are described (in the form in which they were described above) as 'unmanaged' switches. Newer, 'managed' switches (which generally have larger microprocessors, more memory, and increased throughput (the amount of data that can traverse the network in a given timeframe)) offer more functionality. Some examples of this are the ability to provide added security features such as MAC address filtering, DHCP snooping, and monitoring ports. Other such new features may address security and network structure such as vLANs. As mentioned earlier, some 'managed' switches offer a stacking capability, whereby using a proprietary link cable (such as the 'Matrix' cable with 3com Superstack switches), or a plain patch/crossover cable between the uplink ports of the switches, a 'stack' of switches can be managed as one, effectively sharing configuration and management interface.

Some very high-end switches, such as the Cisco 6500 series and the 3com Corebuilder switches also have 'routing engines', which allow them to fulfill some of the functionality of routers. This, again, leads to more 'blur' between the OSI Layers when we come to apply them to 'real life'.

Switches range from small four-port units often integrated with other network devices, and sold as consumer appliances (such as the Linksys WRT54G) to large, high-availability units designed for use in data centers, which support many hundreds of concurrent clients and have an extremely high throughput.

Within the context of this book, we will consider switches in a fairly simple context, and ignore functionality such as vLANs and routing engines, which are outside the scope of what we can reasonably deal with while talking about IPCop (such discussion would more be suited to a book on networking). For the purposes of this book, although a knowledge of switches is useful, it should suffice to understand that switches are *devices that allow all clients plugged into a network socket to talk to every other host on the switch, and as such, provide connectivity for a number of hosts to each other, to a network, and to shared resources stored on servers.*

Routers

If a series of switches and hubs connect together our client devices in order to form a network, routers are, very simply, devices that connect those networks together (put another way, routers are the foundation of inter-networking). A small router (such as a 1700-series Cisco router) may link a branch office to a main office via an ISDN or broadband link, while at the other end of the scale, an expensive high-end router from Cisco, Juniper, or Nortel (or based on an operating system like Windows 2003 or Linux) may have several network links and be responsible for linking a smaller ISP with several larger ISPs it uses to connect to the internet backbone. At the high end of the scale, dedicated devices, although based on architectures similar to PCs, can handle far more traffic than a 'normal' computer running an OS such as Windows or Linux, and as such, these 'backbone' routers are very rarely anything but dedicated devices.

On a TCP/IP network, computers on the same 'subnet' (i.e. plugged into the same hub/switch, or series of hubs/switches) will communicate directly with each other, using ARP (Address Resolution Protocol) to find out the hardware (or MAC) address of the destination computer (as we mentioned when discussing OSI Layers, ARP is used to essentially step between layers two and three), and then sending data directly to this MAC address on the local network segment. It is for this reason that a 'subnet mask' is important; it allows a device to calculate which network addresses are 'local', and which are not. If our network uses the (private) address range 192.168.0.1, and our subnet mask is 255.255.255.0 (or one class C network or a /24 CIDR address space), then any network address not starting with 192.168.0. will be considered as a remote address, and rather than attempting to connect to it directly (via layer two), the device will consult a 'routing table' to see which 'router' should be used to send the data through (via layer three), as an intermediary to another network.

A fairly typical configuration for clients on smaller networks (or well-structured larger networks) is that there is only one router—the 'default' router—through which traffic goes. Using the previous example, if our device attempts to connect to another device at network address 192.0.2.17, the operating system—seeing that this is not a local device according to the network address and subnet of the network adapter—will send data for this destination to the 'default gateway', which then 'routes' the traffic to the correct destination. Although it is possible to configure a client to use different routers for different network segments, this is a more advanced and less common configuration option.

One may want to configure clients with multiple routes if, for instance, a network uses a fast network connection such as an ADSL router as the default gateway (for Internet access), and a slower network connection with a separate router to access another subnet of the internal network (for instance, a branch office of a company that has multiple sites). A preferable scenario for this in a smaller company would be to provide the internal and internet connectivity through one router that handled both, making client configuration and administration simpler (with all traffic via a default gateway, rather than static routing tables on every client pointing to different routers), but this may not always be possible or desirable.

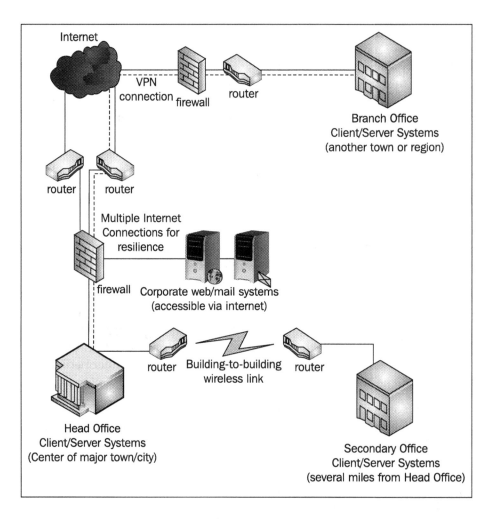

In the above illustration, we consider a company with a head office building. The **Head Office** LAN Infrastructure (represented here by the colonnaded building at the bottom left-hand corner) contains internally accessed servers such as file, mail, print, and directory servers, as well as clients. Situated in between this network and both the Internet and the non-trusted network segment, or DMZ (in which are contained the externally accessible corporate web/mail systems, hosting the corporate website and accepting incoming email) is a firewall.

In addition to clients at the head office situated behind the firewall, we also have a **Secondary Office**, in the same town as the head office — opened when the head office ran out of space for expansion. This office has both server and client systems on the same logical network infrastructure as the **Head Office**, but in its own (routed) subnet, connected to the head office network via a building-to-building wireless link, possibly working by either microwave or laser link.

A **Branch Office** (perhaps for sales staff in another part of the country with a high density of customers for our fictitious business) also uses resources on the **Head Office** network. Due to the distance, this office also has its own servers (most likely file, print, and email systems with content and information being synchronized to the corresponding systems in **Head Office**). In a subnet of its own, this network is linked via VPN, with the route from **Secondary Office** segment to **Head Office** segment tunneled over the Internet and through firewalls due to the prohibitive cost of a leased line or similar connection.

Due to web/mail services being made available to the Internet, our **Head Office** has multiple Internet connections for redundancy. In a scenario like this, there would frequently be several more routers employed both for the **Head Office** infrastructure (which may be fairly large) and for the Internet service provision (and the **Head Office** firewall itself would most likely be, or be accompanied by, another router). These have been omitted for simplicity!

For our purposes, we will consider a router to be a *device that forwards packets across a wide area network or inter-network to their correct destination.*

Routers, Firewalls, and NAT

Although it is easy to talk about networks in such cut and dry terms — separate networks based on layers, and network devices as isolated, well-defined items, this is quite frequently not the case. For many reasons, including network topology and limited resources, roles are quite frequently combined, particularly in smaller networks. Frequently, the first of these to be combined are the roles of 'firewall' and 'router'.

As networks are frequently joined together by routers, this natural choke point can seem a convenient place to firewall as well. This in itself is good networking theory, but frequently this is implemented by adding firewalling functionality or rule sets to the existing router without any change to the network. Although on a small network this makes some sense, it can cause problems in handling load, and adds complexity to a device (router) that should be kept as simple as possible. In general, it is a good idea to split roles wherever possible, by utilizing separate routers, firewalls, proxy servers, etc.

This also applies to other infrastructure roles on servers—DNS servers, Kerberos Domain Controllers, DHCP servers, web servers, and so on, should be kept apart as far as possible, in the interests of performance, reliability, and security.

Unfortunately, as we've already mentioned, this isn't always possible, and there are several network roles that are frequently combined, such as firewalls and routers. Particularly in organizations that do not have their own routable IP addresses for every network device (which is virtually every SME (Small and Medium Enterprise)), there is a need for Network Address Translation. NAT is a process whereby (in order to alleviate the increasing shortage of IP addresses available for use on the Internet), a local network will not use IP addresses that work (are 'routable') on the Internet.

Network Address Translation

Network Address Translation is another consequence of the way in which the Internet and the protocols it is built upon were designed. Much as protocols such as DNS, SMTP, and TCP/IP were designed in an environment in which security was frequently an afterthought, so too was the extent to which (what would become) the Internet would grow. The IPv4 addressing scheme, which we should be familiar with, uses four octets of numbers, each with a range of 0 to 255, a hypothetical maximum of just over four billion addresses (255^4, to be precise).

Given the wide proliferation of internet connectivity and the vast number of personal computers, mobile telephones, PDAs, and other devices that use IP addresses (of which routers, non-mobile IP telephones, and even appliances such as fridges and microwaves are just a few), this address space although initially probably considered huge, is beginning to run out. For this reason, and as a result of the long timeframe for deployment of IPv6 (which aside from many other functional improvements upon IPv4 includes a larger address space), an interim method was required in order to reduce the rate at which IP addresses were being consumed—this is NAT.

As an example of how NAT is used in practice, consider the following hypothetical scenario:

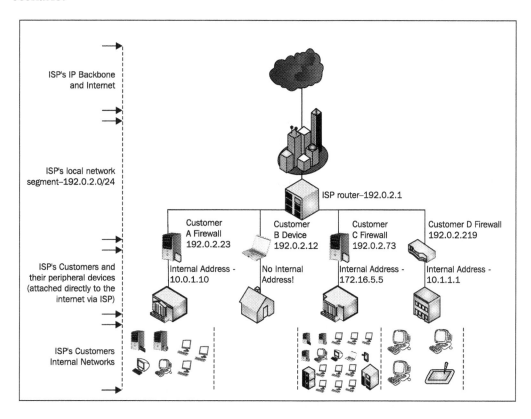

Consider the diagram above—a fictional ISP and four of its customers. Each customer is allocated one IP address by the ISP, assigned to the computer or device directly attached to the connection provided by the ISP.

Customer A is a medium-sized solicitors firm—Customer A has a firewall based on IPCop, several servers, and several clients in its private network segment. It uses the 10.0.1.0/24 (class C) subnet for its internal clients, but its external IP is actually used by several dozen computers.

Customer B is a home user—customer B has only one computer, a laptop, which is directly attached to the ISP's internet connection. Customer B's external IP is used by one computer, and has no NAT and no private internal network.

Customer C is a larger manufacturing company—customer C has a high-end firewall attached to its internet connection, and a large number of diverse devices in its internal network. Customer C uses the 172.16.5.0/24 subnet for the network segment directly behind its firewall, and has a phone system, clients, server systems, and a midrange mainframe system in its internal network.

Customer D is a home with several computers for members of the family, and a tablet PC—they have a handful of clients attached to a wireless network provided by an all-in-one switch/router/firewall device (possibly the Linksys WAP54G mentioned earlier) purchased at a local computer store.

Just four IP addresses actually represent hundreds of clients on the Internet—through clever use of technology, clients using Internet Service Providers to provide access to the Internet reduce IP wastage by not allocating an IP address for every host.

If your computer exists as a host on a network on which the default gateway is performing Network Address Translation, and you visit a website, your computer will initiate a connection to port 80 on the web server you are connecting to, your computer will send a packet of data from the IP address it has (in the case of NAT, a private address like 192.168.1.23) to the destination. The destination will, in the case of a website on the Internet, be an internet-routable IP address such as 72.14.207.99 (one of Google's IP addresses).

If your gateway simply forwarded this packet to Google, it would be unlikely to get there in the first place, as a router between your computer and Google would almost certainly be configured to 'drop' packets from addresses like the 192.168.0.0/16 address range, which are not valid for internet communications. Instead, therefore, your router *rewrites* the packet before forwarding it, and swaps the 192.168.1.23 for the external address of your router, given to you temporarily by your ISP.

When replies come back from the host at the other end, the router, having made a note of the translation process, consults a table in memory, establishes based on the sequence number of the connection that 192.168.1.23 was the originating host, and rewrites the packet back again. Effectively, your clients are masquerading as the device attached to the Internet (or it is masquerading as them), and indeed, 'masquerading' is the technical term used for NAT in the iptables/netfilter firewalling components in Linux. Although the NAT process breaks some more complicated protocols, it is an extremely effective way of having many hundreds or thousands of devices online behind one internet-routable (public) IP address.

For the clients, the setup appears as if their address range existed as a normal, routed segment of the Internet, whereas in actual fact, the 'default gateway' is performing Network Address Translation. In this manner, the worldwide shortage of IP addresses is alleviated at the expense of some convenience. Small and home office devices in particular, such as any of those marketed by D-Link, Linksys et al., almost always use Network Address Translation to provide connectivity to their clients, and IPCop uses it too.

Private Address Ranges

These 'private' IP address ranges are set out in RFC 1918 (http://www.rfc-archive.org/getrfc.php?rfc=1918). RFCs, or Requests For Comment, while not technical standards, are "*technical and organizational notes about the Internet (originally the ARPANET), beginning in 1969. Memos in the RFC series discuss many aspects of computer networking, including protocols, procedures, programs, and concepts, as well as meeting notes, opinions, and sometimes humor.*" (http://www.rfc-editor.org/, front page, November 20, 2005). For protocols, standards, and convention, they make an excellent first line of reference, although (often depending upon the authors and intended audience) they are usually fairly technical.

The most recognizable of the private IP ranges is probably the 192.168.0.0/16 range, which constitutes 255 class C 'subnets', of which the two most commonly used are the 192.168.0.1/24 and the 192.168.1.1/24 subnets. This address range is very frequently used as the default private address range for **Small Office Home Office (SOHO)** routers. There are also two other private address ranges for these purposes, the 10.0.0.0/8 and 172.16.0.0/12 ranges.

Combined Role Devices

As a result of NAT, devices at the border of Small Office Home Office Networks, therefore, are almost always *combined-role*, and although typically marketed as *router/firewalls* or simply *routers*, often perform all of the following roles:

- Router (performing Network Address Translation)
- Firewall
- DHCP server
- Caching / Resolving DNS server

Some such devices (including IPCop) may also provide some of the following pieces of functionality, most of which are generally more commonly found in enterprise products:

- Proxy server
- Content Filtering
- File server

- Intrusion Detection
- VPN/IPSec server

Due to the complex nature of some of these tasks, it is often the case that the 'embedded' combined devices are difficult to configure and interoperating some of the more complex functions (such as IPSec and File Serving) with other devices (such as an IPSec/VPN device from another vendor) can be very difficult. Although the price and size of these devices makes them a very attractive prospect for smaller networks, networks requiring some of the more advanced functionality should look at them quite carefully and evaluate whether or not, economically and technically, they will meet their needs.

When combined roles are required, larger, more fully designed solutions (such as a firewall appliance from Borderware, Checkpoint, Cisco, et al.) or commercial piece of software (such as Microsoft's ISA server) often do the job more effectively and in a manner more configurable and interoperable than their smaller, cheaper SOHO cousins. Obviously, we believe that not only does IPCop do a better job at the tasks it is intended for than embedded devices, but than some of the commercial firewall and gateway packages as well!

Traffic Filtering

Knowing what firewalls are intended to do and why their function is important to us, it is now necessary to explore, briefly, how it is that firewalls accomplish the broad purpose we've assigned for them.

Personal Firewalls

Personal firewalls have become increasingly common in the last five years. With the inclusion of personal firewalling technology in Windows XP Service Pack 2 (and augmented technology in the upcoming Windows Vista), as well as firewalling stacks in the OSX and Linux operating systems, it is now a fairly normal occurrence for workstations and desktops to be running firewalling software.

Generally, this comes in one of two forms—either firewalling software built into the operating system (as in the case of OSX, Linux, and XP's Windows Firewall), or one of the many third-party firewalls from software vendors who write such software. Two relatively well regarded examples of such packages are Agnitum's Outpost package and ZoneLabs ZoneAlarm package.

Personal firewalling software cannot be a true firewall. As we have discussed earlier, a firewall is a security boundary between one side of the firewall and another. By definition, a personal firewall must accept data onto a computer before making the decision as to whether it is allowed to be there or not. Many forms of exploit involve the misinterpretation of maliciously crafted data while parsing and evaluating that data. Since a firewall is performing these tasks on the host it is supposed to be protecting, there is no way in which it can effectively isolate the portions of the software that are doing the protecting from the portions of the software that are being protected. Even for a smaller network, a personal firewall can never offer the degree of segregation that a network firewall provides.

Although personal firewalling software is relatively effective against inbound (ingress) traffic, such software cannot offer protection against unauthorized outbound (or egress) traffic, since an application generating such traffic on the workstation will typically have some degree of access to the firewall's internals. If the logged on user is an administrator of the workstation (or if there exists a security flaw in the operating system allowing a non-administrative application to gain system or administrative privileges), it is quite possible to circumvent software/personal firewalls using the operating system (`http://www.vigilantminds.com/files/defeating_windows_personal_firewalls.pdf`) in a way that simply isn't possible with a firewall distinct from the client itself.

Many personal firewall packages, such as ZoneAlarm, step beyond the services offered solely by a packet filtering firewall, and serve as a Host-based Intrusion Detection System (HIDS) or Host-based Intrusion Prevention System (HIPS). These systems actively monitor, and in the case of a HIPS, prevent, alterations to the operating system and its components. Such functions cannot be provided by a network firewall such as IPCop for obvious reasons, but the same criticisms apply to a HIPS as to a Personal Firewall—ultimately, if the host it is running on is compromised, the accuracy of the Intrusion Prevention System is compromised also.

Recent developments in security include rootkit software, which is capable of providing a 'backdoor' into a host operating system using virtualization software (such as VMware) and hardware-based virtualization support (such as that in AMD and Intel's newest processors). Such software, like VMware and Virtual PC themselves, literally acts as a container (or hypervisor) for the OS running inside it, the consequence of which is that such backdoors literally exist outside the OS that installed them. In light of these concepts being demonstrated publicly, the role of host-based firewall and IPS software is redoubled—part of a security solution, but not a 'killer app'. Fundamentally, what we can take from this that is for sure is that different packages have different strengths, and we shouldn't ever rely on one in particular.

Although an important part of an overall stance on security, not all firewalls are created equal, and a personal firewall should never be considered to be a substitute for well-designed, well-maintained perimeter and segment firewalling as part of a network's overall security strategy.

Stateless Packet Filtering

'Packet filtering' is a term generally used to describe a firewall, acting at the network layer, which decides where data should go based on criteria from the data packet. Generally, this will include the source and destination ports and source and destination addresses—so, for instance, an organization may allow connections to its remote access server from a business partner's IP address range but not from the Internet in general. Other criteria may include the time of day at which the connection is made.

Although fast and historically effective, 'stateless' packet filters operate solely at the network layer and provide no inspection of data traveling through them at all—a stateless packet filter configured to allow traffic from the Internet to port 80 in an organization's DMZ will allow such traffic, irrespective of what the data going to port 80 is, and more importantly whether or not that data is actually part of an established connection.

Stateful Packet Filtering

A packet filter that is stateful understands the state of a TCP connection that is in progress through it. When a TCP Connection is set up a very specific process known as a 'three-way handshake' takes place between the source and the target hosts.

This is a very basic, simplistic explanation of stateful firewalling—it would be out of scope for this text to cover the entire topic of stateful firewalling (there are other resources such as http://en.wikipedia.org/wiki/Stateful_inspection that cover this), but a basic explanation of the topic is useful:

Firstly, the client in the connection issues a TCP SYN packet to the destination. For the firewall, this is considered a 'new' connection, and at this point the firewall will allocate memory to track the status of the connection as it progresses.

Secondly, the server—if the connection proceeds as expected—replies by sending back a packet with the correct sequence number, source, and destination ports, with both SYN and ACK flags set.

Thirdly, the client, upon receiving the SYN ACK packet, returns a third packet with solely the ACK packet set. Frequently, this packet will also contain some of the first bits of data pertaining to the connection in it. At this point, the firewall considers the connection to be 'established', and will allow data associated with this connection (that is to say, data to and from the source/destination addresses, going to and from the correct ports, with the correct sequence number) to freely pass through the firewall.

In the event that this is not completed, the firewall will forget about the details of the connection either after a specific time period or when the available memory to remember such connections is exhausted, depending upon how the firewall works. This added use of memory makes 'stateful' packet inspection more processor and memory intensive, although as it only inspects the header of our data, it is still not as processor or memory-intensive as a firewall that inspects data all of the way up to the application layer and so unpacks the payload of data packets traversing it also.

The principle advantage of a stateful firewall, however, stems from the understanding it has of 'established' connections. In a network with several clients with a non-stateful firewall that allows those clients to connect to external sites on port 80, any traffic with a destination port of 80 will be allowed out of the network, but more importantly, any host on the Internet will be able to bypass the firewall completely and connect to internal clients simply by sending their traffic from a source port of 80. Because responses from web servers will come from port 80, without the firewall checking to see if connections from outside the network from port 80 are responses to internal clients (i.e. without acting statefully), there is no way to prevent this.

A stateful firewall, however, will only allow data to traverse the firewall if it is part of an 'established' connection. Since there should be no payload allowed through for packets that are sent before the three-way handshake, this minimizes what an attacker could actually do to a target system without fully connecting to it in a way allowed by the firewall.

Application-Layer Firewalling

Although stateful packet firewalls can very effectively restrict where traffic can go to and from on a network, it cannot control what exactly that traffic is. The actual data inside data packets themselves exists at a higher level than packet firewalls, which as network-layer devices are unaware of the application layer.

As an example of this, consider a simple office network with a gateway that allows connections outbound to port 80 (HTTP) in order to allow clients on the network to browse the Internet. The network administrator has denied connections to all other ports such as 443 and 25, as the company policy dictates that staff should not be able to access external mail (via 25) or sites that require HTTPS login (as many of these are sites such as eBay and webmail sites, which the company does not want its staff to access). It uses a stateful firewall in order to prevent traffic coming into its network with a source port of 80, which might be used to attack, probe, or scan clients on its network.

This firewall, however, does not prevent staff from accessing other resources on port 80—one of the staff might, for instance, have set up a mail server listening on port

80 and be using this to read his or her mail. Another might have the SSH service or a VPN server running on a server outside the company or at home listening to port 80 and use this connection to 'tunnel' other traffic through in order to connect to services (such as mail, IRC, etc.) that the IT policy denies.

This is extremely hard to prevent unless the administrator has a firewall that understands the application layer, because only then can he or she restrict traffic based specifically on what sort of traffic it is. Such firewalls are often called 'proxy firewalls', because the way in which they function is frequently by proxying traffic—accepting the connection on behalf of the client, unpacking it and inspecting the data, and then forwarding it on to the destination if it is allowed by whatever access control the firewall has in place. As with stateful firewalls, an application-layer firewall or proxy server may restrict traffic based on destination, time, content, (in this case), and many other factors. Squid, the open-source proxy server that ships with IPCop, is very powerful in this respect, and has the ability to enforce powerful access control, particularly in conjunction with the Squidguard add-on.

Web proxy servers, debatably, are a frequently deployed application-layer firewall— although not often considered as such, many proxy servers have functionality that approximates that of a full-fledged application-layer firewall, and by blocking normal connections to port 80 and forcing connections to the Internet through a proxy server, organizations ensure that requests made to port 80 are HTTP, and no other protocol is allowed over that port. Unfortunately, many protocols (such as SSL on port 443) are very hard to proxy due to their use of cryptography, and for this reason these ports are frequently unprotected and therefore are good candidates for a malicious intruder (or errant employee) to use for nefarious purposes.

Consider border control as an object lesson—we restrict cross-border travel by using passports to verify whether someone is authorized to go to and from a source and destination country—this is analogous to stateless packet filtering, as passports are similar in nature to packet headers; they contain information about the bearer (or payload). We then use visas to verify the *state* of someone during their travel—that is to say, whether they are in the state of being at the end of their legitimate stay, having no legitimate reason to enter the country (even though by law they may be entitled to), and so on. The passport (and inspection of it) by itself does not restrict travel based on who someone is and what they are doing, as well as whether they are on a blacklist or not for security reasons. This is analogous to application-layer firewalling. Further, through passports and lists, governments inspect the people themselves who travel cross-border, and examine their bags (their payload) to verify whether it is legitimately carried (or contains contraband, such as explosives or munitions)—this could be compared both to application-layer firewalls and Intrusion Detection / Prevention Systems.

Proxy Servers

Proxy servers, then, can be a form of application-layer firewalling. A proxy server is, very simply, a device that accepts a request from one computer, and passes it to another. In passing the request along, a proxy server may also levy certain restrictions upon exactly what that request can be. Most importantly, however, as a proxy server understands the concept of a 'request', it provides security over and above simply allowing a client to connect to the destination server or service itself, as a proxy server will not allow just anything to traverse the firewall.

Consider our earlier example — the small network that wishes to allow clients to access the Internet, while preventing them from accessing certain resources (such as mail, online auction sites, games, etc.). The network administrator, deciding that the present firewalling strategy is inadequate, installs a proxy server, and configures the web browser for clients on the network (either by hand, or automatically using a script or a centralized configuration method such as Red Hat Directory server or Microsoft's Active Directory) to point to the proxy server for Internet access.

The network administrator then configures the firewall to drop all outbound connections from workstations on the network (allowing connections to the Internet from the proxy server). At this point, if anyone is using the gateway/firewall to connect to the Internet, such as a hypothetical employee connecting to an SSH server on port 80 for nefarious purposes, those connections will be dropped by the firewall (and possibly logged). From this point onwards, whenever an employee initiates a connection to a website using his or her web browser, the web browser does not do what it had done previously and attempt to connect to the website in question and retrieve content for the user. Instead, the web browser connects to the proxy server it has been configured with, and requests that the proxy server give it the webpage in question.

It is at this point that a proxy server enacting any form of access control would determine whether the user in question was allowed to access the requested resource it. Dan's Guardian is an example of a package for IPCop that allows the filtering of inappropriate websites.

Another advantage of proxy servers is that as they act as a chokepoint for the **requests** for content, they can check to see if a webpage has been requested already, and if it has, then give the client a local (cached) copy of the page, instead of retrieving another copy of the same content. Such proxy servers are referred to as *caching web proxies*. Microsoft's ISA server, and the Open Source package Squid are both examples of these.

Having established that there is no local copy of the content (if the proxy server is caching) and that the user is authorized to view the content (if there is access control in effect), the proxy server will attempt to retrieve the content itself, either from an upstream proxy server, or (more likely) from the Internet itself. The proxy server may return an error to the user if the destination site does not exist, or give an error returned from the remote site to the user.

Transparent proxies (which IPCop has support for), or *'intercepting proxies'* (`http://www.rfc.org.uk/cgi-bin/lookup.cgi?rfc=rfc3040`)' perform this via NAT without the need for reconfiguration (and without the required participation of the client), taking advantage of chokepoints to impose network policy upon traffic.

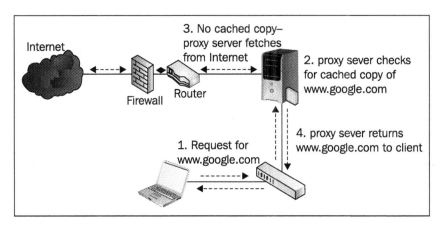

In the example above, our transparent proxy server fetches `www.google.com` for a laptop client. Hypothetically, we allow access to most internet sites (such as Google) but block access to sites with keywords such as "pornography" or which are contained on a blacklist. In this situation, the proxy server accomplishes the goals of our IT Policy by providing content filtering. It also sanitizes the content to ensure that only valid HTTP traffic is allowed, and not connections for arbitrary applications (such as Skype or MSN), which our IT Policy disallows. If a second client now requests the same page, the proxy server can deliver the cached copy (eliminating step 3) significantly quicker than the first time around, delivering a better service for clients and reducing the load on the internet connection. The proxy server essentially does the 'heavy lifting' for the client itself.

In a firewalling role, the principle advantage of a proxy server, aside from the ability to more effectively restrict users from accessing certain resources, is the fact that it sanitizes, to a certain degree, data going into and out of the network. Since in order for traffic to go out of, or come into, the network it must conform to the standards pertaining to web pages, which a web proxy understands, 'out of band' or non-standard data is significantly harder to get into/out of the security perimeter.

Some packages, such as the open-source package Zorp and Microsoft's ISA server, will also proxy other protocols, such as RPC—this is a relatively new entrant to the firewalling world, and it is less common to see firewalls deployed with this sort of functionality outside enterprise networks.

Other Services Sometimes Run on Firewalls

Although in enterprise scenarios (such as the example of network topology listed earlier in this chapter) firewalls, routers, and proxy servers are generally separate devices, in smaller networks (and even some larger ones), roles are very frequently combined. Even in a large enterprise, in our branch office, it might not make economic sense to have three network infrastructure servers (firewall, router, proxy server) and three desktop infrastructure servers (fileserver, mail server, print server) if the office only has a staff of 50! By putting all of our network tasks on one host running something such as IPCop, and handling our desktop services off one server, we cut our equipment by 2/3, and possibly improve performance (since we can put those services on higher-specification machines). Our easier-to-manage environment requires less electricity, reduced air conditioning, and takes up less space.

DNS

DNS, the Domain Name System (http://www.dns.net/dnsrd/rfc/), is the system used across the Internet (and on private networks) to translate hostnames into IP addresses. As with previous topics, this is a very basic, simplistic explanation of what DNS does—this is designed to give a basic understanding of the topic, and not breed DNS experts. There have been many books written on the theory and practicalities of DNS (http://www.packtpub.com/DNS/book being one such example), and it is outside our scope to recreate them here.

In addition to a default gateway and/or proxy server for internet access, clients are assigned a DNS server, which allows them to look up an Internet Protocol address for any given DNS domain name. When a connection is made to another host, a network client will issue a lookup request to the first DNS server that it has been assigned, asking for an A record (unless it is connecting to a service such as SMTP, which uses its own specific record, in this instance MX, for configuration).

The DNS server returns to the client an IP address, or more than one IP address, which the client then uses to connect to the site via the default gateway or to issue a request to the proxy server for connectivity. In many instances there is one IP address defined as the A record for a website, which the client will connect to, but in some instances, typically for larger sites, there are several—in these instances, they will be returned in a random order by the responding DNS server each time they are requested, using this order to balance traffic across all of the IP addresses. This technique is known as "round-robin DNS", and a prime example of a site using this is Google.

Email uses MX records to indicate where email for a particular domain should go to. Each MX record listed for a domain will typically have its own 'preference number'—convention is that the lowest preference number is the most important mail server, so it is quite a frequent occurrence for a domain name to have two (or more) MX records set up, a primary (with a priority of, for instance, 10) for a main mail server, and a secondary (with a priority of, for instance, 50) pointing to a backup MX server in case the primary is down.

Using the `dig` or `host` commands on a Unix or Linux system (or a Windows system with the cygwin toolkit installed), or using the `nslookup` command in Windows (or Unix/Linux), we can retrieve the IP addresses listed for a given domain name and (with a recent version of the `host` command) the MX records for it, like so:

```
james@horus: ~ $ host google.com
google.com has address 72.14.207.99
google.com has address 64.233.187.99
google.com mail is handled by 10 smtp2.google.com.
google.com mail is handled by 10 smtp3.google.com.
google.com mail is handled by 10 smtp4.google.com.
google.com mail is handled by 10 smtp1.google.com.
james@horus: ~ $
```

The `dig` command (which takes as input the type of record to retrieve as the first argument) can also be used to troubleshoot this, as follows:

```
james@horus: ~ $ dig mx google.com

; <<>> DiG 9.3.1 <<>> mx google.com
;; global options:  printcmd
;; Got answer:
;; ->>HEADER<<- opcode: QUERY, status: NOERROR, id: 64387
;; flags: qr rd ra; QUERY: 1, ANSWER: 4, AUTHORITY: 0, ADDITIONAL: 1

;; QUESTION SECTION:
;google.com.                    IN      MX

;; ANSWER SECTION:
google.com.             118     IN      MX      10 smtp3.google.com.
google.com.             118     IN      MX      10 smtp4.google.com.
google.com.             118     IN      MX      10 smtp1.google.com.
google.com.             118     IN      MX      10 smtp2.google.com.
```

```
;; ADDITIONAL SECTION:
smtp3.google.com.       209      IN      A       64.233.183.25

;; Query time: 21 msec
;; SERVER: 10.1.1.6#53(10.1.1.6)
;; WHEN: Sun Nov 20 19:59:24 2005
;; MSG SIZE  rcvd: 132

james@horus: ~ $
```

As a perfect demonstration of round-robin DNS, we can see that the MX records were returned in a different order (2341, 3412) each time we queried for them, spreading out the load among them.

The nslookup command in Windows may be used as follows in interactive mode to look up MX records (or A records, which are the default, without setting an explicit record type) as follows:

```
Windows PowerShell                                                    _ □ ×
PS C:\> nslookup
*** Can't find server name for address 10.1.2.1: Non-existent domain
*** Default servers are not available
Default Server:  UnKnown
Address:  10.1.2.1

> set type=mx
> google.com
Server:  UnKnown
Address:  10.1.2.1

Non-authoritative answer:
google.com      MX preference = 10, mail exchanger = smtp2.google.com
google.com      MX preference = 10, mail exchanger = smtp3.google.com
google.com      MX preference = 10, mail exchanger = smtp4.google.com
google.com      MX preference = 10, mail exchanger = smtp1.google.com

smtp3.google.com         internet address = 64.233.183.25
smtp4.google.com         internet address = 66.102.9.25
smtp1.google.com         internet address = 216.239.57.25
smtp2.google.com         internet address = 64.233.167.25
> _
```

This knowledge can often be useful when troubleshooting firewall and networking problems, as DNS failure is one of many problems that can prevent connectivity (and is virtually the number one cause of malfunctions in misconfigured Active Directory environments). Knowledge of DNS (and how to look up DNS records manually) and knowing how to use the ping command are the first two tools in the IT Professional's toolkit for debugging connectivity issues. The ping command is often useful for troubleshooting connectivity, although frequently the layer-four protocol that ping uses, ICMP, is firewalled either at the client side or at the destination (www.microsoft.com is an example of a website that drops ICMP packets), so the lack of a ping response cannot always be relied upon as a clear indicator of connectivity issues.

IPCop includes a DNS server, which, set up by default, acts as a resolving name server — that is to say, it will accept DNS requests from clients and resolve them externally, passing the results back to clients on the local network. As with a web proxy server, this can speed up requests when the resolving name server has a cached copy of the domain/IP correlation, which it can pass back to a client without the added milliseconds of resolving it fully. Clients can also be configured to make their own DNS queries through the firewall to an external DNS server, but this is inefficient, opens unnecessary ports through the firewall, and is generally not a recommended configuration.

DHCP

DHCP, the Dynamic Host Configuration Protocol, is a descendant of BOOTP, an earlier protocol, and is used to configure hosts on a network automatically with network addresses and other configuration information, such as gateway and DNS server information. DHCP works using broadcast traffic — very simply, a client configured to use DHCP sends out a UDP packet with a DHCPDISCOVER message to the address 255.255.255.255 (a broadcast address, forwarded to every host in the same subnet) when it connects to a network, requesting a DHCP server.

Based on the client's request, a DHCP server on the network segment will send a DHCPOFFER request back, specifying an IP address it offers to the client. Generally speaking, a client will only be offered one IP address by one server (it's fairly rare for more than one DHCP server to be running on the same network segment), but in the event that there is more than one server, the client will pick one of the offered IP addresses. The client then returns a DHCPREQUEST message to the broadcast address, requesting the configuration it has picked. All things going well, the server returns a DHCPACK message to the client to confirm that it can have the assigned configuration information.

DHCP, in addition to an IP address, is also capable of assigning a variety of other configuration information, the most common few options being DNS servers, WINS servers, Gateway, Subnet Mask, NTP servers, and DNS Domain Name. IPCop includes a DHCP implementation configured by default to hand out the requisite information to use the IPCop server for internet access, and uses *Dynamic DNS* to populate the DNS server with hostnames sent out by DHCP requests, such that there are DNS entries set up for clients on the network when they request configuration via DHCP.

DHCP configuration (or static network configuration) can be viewed on a client device in Windows using the 'ipconfig /a' command or, in Unix/Linux, using the 'ifconfig -a' command. In Windows, the ipconfig command also allows the user to release and renew DHCP information.

Summary

In this chapter, we have covered topics like where the Internet came from, some of the design considerations that went into it, and why firewalls are important and fit into the grand scheme of things. We also took a look at basic networking, including how network layers are significant and what they do, some different types of firewall, and some other services firewalls may operate.

We should by this point have a relatively good understanding of the scope of the protocols and technology used in IPCop. We may also have identified some technologies that you hadn't heard of or didn't understand—don't worry, this is a good thing! If so inclined, there is plenty of scope to learn about these technologies based on the information summarized here and the links given to other resources.

2
Introduction to IPCop

Before we look at how we use IPCop, we need to first look at the background of IPCop and the tools it is built with. We also need to look at the licenses those tools are distributed under, and therefore the IPCop license. This chapter will be less beneficial for those who would like to get straight to the installation and configuration and already know the background of open-source software, the GPL, and Linux. We will, however, also look at the reasons to choose IPCop in this chapter and the unique features it has, which will be useful when deciding whether to or how to deploy IPCop. It is, therefore, extremely important.

Free and Open Source Software

Many people might have heard of several common types of software, such as freeware, which is software you are allowed to use for free and (more generically), commercial software such as Microsoft Windows or Adobe Photoshop. Commercial software, generally, comes with a license restricting you to use the software in a certain way, and usually banning you from copying or modifying it.

IPCop is a type of software known as **Open Source Software** (**OSS**). As a piece of OSS, IPCop is released under a license called the **GNU General Public License** (**GPL**).

As with all Open Source Software packages distributed under this license and others like it, IPCop affords its users some basic freedoms.

Under the GPL, IPCop users are given the freedom to read, modify, and redistribute the source code of the software. The only caveat attached to this is that if you decide to redistribute this software (for instance, if you make a copy of IPCop with some improvements and give it to a friend) you must provide the modified work under the same license, and provide access to the source code. As we will see when we look at the history of IPCop, this can be very beneficial for users who would like to take a project in a new direction.

The GPL is one of the best-known open-source licenses. There are many others, however, such as the **Berkeley Software Distribution License** (**BSD License**). Each license differs in exactly what freedom it gives you, but all of them must allow at least the ability to read, modify, and redistribute the source code in order to be considered an open-source license by the Open Source Initiative.

What is Source Code?

Source code is a set of instructions written by a computer programmer in a human-readable language. This set of instructions is usually then converted by a **compiler** into an executable program that the computer can run. With closed-source software such as Microsoft Windows and ISA Server, you don't get to see this. With Open Source Software such as Linux and IPCop, you do!

The Open Source Initiative is a non-profit organization involved in promoting open-source software and aiding developers in creating and using open-source licenses. It also maintains a list of all licenses accepted as open source.

You can find all of the licenses recognized by the Open Source Initiative at `http://www.opensource.org/`.

The GPL itself can be found on the GNU website, `http://www.gnu.org/copyleft/gpl.html`.

In addition to being the best-known OSS license, the GPL is also the license chosen by the best-known piece of OSS, the Linux kernel, which is a key component of IPCop. The release of the Linux kernel under the GPL is what makes systems like IPCop possible. The Linux kernel is the core of a Linux-based operating system (such as any of the Linux distributions that are variants of GNU/Linux). The kernel is developed by a team of developers mostly comprising volunteers around the world, but including many developers who are paid by companies that rely on Linux for some of their business, such as Red Hat Linux, Canonical, IBM, Novell, and Sun Microsystems.

As we are now aware, creating Open Source Software means giving our users the ability to modify our source code and then redistribute their modifications. This is what has been done with IPCop. IPCop has taken the Linux kernel as well as a large number of other tools, bundled them into a **distribution** of software and enabled users to create a feature-rich easy-to-use firewall system. This is how a lot of Open Source Software is created and is a function of the philosophy behind OSS.

Forking IPCop

Not only can you build your software on top of other components with OSS, but you can take it a step further and take one of those components (or a collection of those — called a **distribution**) and modify it to become something that suits your needs better than the design of the original developers. For example, if the users and developers of a particular piece of software decide they want something more from the software or want the software to be taken in another direction, they have the full freedom to do so. This is what happened with IPCop.

Before IPCop was created, SmoothWall existed (`http://www.smoothwall.org`). SmoothWall is a very similar distribution to IPCop at the present time and all of the initial code in IPCop was SmoothWall code. SmoothWall, however, employed *dual licensing* to release variants of its free firewall commercially. The commercial variants of SmoothWall had greater functionality, possibly causing conflict between the development goals of the free and commercial packages as there is a disincentive to improve a free product if it will cause your non-free product to make less money.

This led to tension between users of the software and some of the developers. The current IPCop developers decided to develop the system based on the work already put in to SmoothWall but they didn't want to follow SmoothWall's current philosophy and direction. As such, there was a decision to create a new branch of the software — to **fork** it. One of the main reasons behind the fork was a desire to create a firewall with the features available in commercial SmoothWall and then release this as a purely non-commercial piece of OSS.

Creating a new branch of software like this is called *forking* for quite obvious reasons. A fork is generally carried out by users and/or current developers by taking a snapshot of the source code and deciding to develop it in a different direction. They add different features, possibly remove some things that are not important for the project, and an alternative piece of software is created, which often competes with the original software, or provides an alternative to it.

Other examples of *forked* software are the many different distributions of the GNU tools and Linux such as Mandrake, Debian, Slackware, Ubuntu, and so on. Some of them are derived from their own packaging of the Linux kernel and GNU tools and some of them are derived from each other. For example Adamantix and Ubuntu are derived from Debian and they feature different design goals from each other and from their parent software.

Forking is also a process that commercial software undergoes — the many different versions of the Windows operating system, for instance, are ultimately forked from the same source code. By *forking* the source code and developing *server* versions of Windows (such as Windows 2003 Server) and *client* versions of Windows (such as Windows XP), Microsoft is better able to provide functionality in each version that is fitting to the purpose of the version, and the price charged for it.

There is a rich diversity of OSS, and without the freedom involved in licensing IPCop itself wouldn't exist, since it is derived from the GNU tools, Linux, SmoothWall, and many other open-source packages. This is by no means an exhaustive list and the number of developers involved in creating all of the code involved in such a system is very hard to estimate.

The license that IPCop is released under means that if a company chooses to use the system internally and subsequently decides that it would like to make some changes to it, it is free to do this—modifications are a right that is taken for granted under the license, and there is no obligation for you to redistribute changes you make that are only used internally. If you do decide to redistribute your modifications (to a friend, partner, or another company), all that is asked is that you afford your users the same benefits you received initially; i.e. if you decide to release the software, then you must release the software under the GPL. The license even makes a provision to charge a (reasonable) distribution fee to cover costs (although the people you redistribute it to are themselves free to redistribute the software to whomever they want, at no cost!). The added power this gives a piece of software is hard to measure, but it is very easy to see how this could be beneficial.

The example of forking in OSS was that of IPCop forking from SmoothWall. There is logically nothing to stop that happening again and in the opinion of the authors, diversity and choice when it comes to software is a good thing.

If we don't yet have a handle on the power of this license, one excellent example is that of highly secure installations. In a situation in which you need complete source code control and the ability to modify software at will to accommodate a secure environment, having IPCop with its source code gives you a firewall that is fully functional from which you can create a more customized system in order to secure your network if you need that sort of flexibility. This can be a change to the kernel underneath the system or changes to the configuration options, or even adding and removing firewall capabilities. Since there is no requirement to redistribute you can decide to keep this fully private and essentially have an in-house system where only a small amount of development investment was needed. There are a lot of software options that offer this and this is one of the biggest benefits OSS such as IPCop has over closed-source and commercial competitors in the marketplace.

If you don't need this flexibility, you still benefit from the developers that did use this flexibility in order to create a very useful system. The open nature of the development process is a direct consequence of the open nature of the code, and the sheer number of people who are able to get their hands on projects such as IPCop, the Linux kernel, or the Apache web server, means that these software packages can be highly polished and kept free of bugs, which commercial products with development teams that are comparatively tiny might not be so assiduous about.

The Purpose of IPCop

IPCop is a firewall for the Small Office/Home Office (SOHO) network, which is extremely easy to use. It provides most of the basic features that you would expect a modern firewall to have, and what is most important is that it sets this all up for you in a highly automated and simplified way. It's very easy to get an IPCop system up and running and takes hardly any time.

For features such as those in IPCop, we would usually have to pay for a high-end firewall system or string something together with a collection of other tools. IPCop takes some of these powerful tools and creates a pre-built package for us.

IPCop was created to fill what appears to be a void in the market, where users with small networks need some features that generally only large networks can afford, as far as the requirement for expertise or money is concerned. This book hopes to provide the additional expertise to make an adequate replacement for a commercial product really shine, as well as give a look at how to set up IPCop in a number of different scenarios.

The Benefits of Building on Stable Components

IPCop could very well be developed as an add-on to an operating system in the way that Shorewall is an application to be installed on a Linux system or ISA server on a Windows system, making it an application you install over your existing setup. You would then be left with the maintenance of the system underlying the software package.

The disadvantage of this is that if your server's purpose is only to be a firewall for your network you would be required to have an adequate basic understanding of the Linux operating system in order to get the software installed and if you want it to perform well you would have to configure both the operating system and IPCop itself. However, since IPCop installs as an operating system of its own, you have no real need to know Linux in order to use the system. When it comes to stability, this means that the IPCop developers can concentrate on one platform for their development and can be completely confident that they are in control of that environment. They are fully responsible for configuring this and when it comes to support they can be relatively sure the users haven't destabilized the system by wrongly configuring the operating system—and if they have, then hopefully they understand the consequences such that they either do it properly or understand why IPCop breaks after they tinker with it!

Stability, security, reliability, and ease of use are probably the most important factors for smaller networks and are the areas in which IPCop, then, seems to excel. Being built on the 2.4 series of the Linux kernel, the system has a noteworthy level of security, stability, and reliability. Also, having tools installed that are used in networks of different sizes around the world provides a massive user base meaning that the systems in use are well-tested and have a lot of individuals and companies using them, reporting bugs on them, and relying on them for their business.

The Linux kernel is one of the largest single pieces of OSS and includes millions of lines of source code developed by a multitude of developers from all over the world. Linux has many modern operating system features such as support for wireless and Bluetooth devices as well as the most current encrypted network communications. As we will see throughout the course of this book, some of these features have become invaluable to the IPCop developers and therefore the IPCop users who benefit from the features that can be included in the IPCop distribution. The developers of IPCop don't have to worry terribly much about lower-level network communication, because they have built IPCop on top of the pre-existing kernel code, which manages this.

This sort of layering — software on top of other software — enables developers to concentrate on the area they know best, and for the IPCop developers, this area is making an easy-to-use firewall. You may find this a concept familiar from the network layering of the OSI model, which we covered in the previous chapter. This interoperability, whether it occurs in an application stack, operating system, or set of network protocols, is crucial to build reliable, secure systems. *Open Standards,* from network protocols like HTTP to document formats like the Open Document Format, are of critical importance to it.

Some of the other software we have mentioned includes Apache and OpenSSH. Apache, the web server that serves the pages used to configure IPCop, powers some of the largest websites in the world. According to the latest web server survey, Apache is used on almost 70% of the world's web servers (`http://news.netcraft.com/archives/2005/11/07/november_2005_web_server_survey.html`).

Apache therefore seems like an extremely stable and trustworthy system and gives the IPCop developers incredible flexibility when working on their user interface, which is almost entirely web-based. Other than the set-up procedure there is no real need to go beyond the web interface. By combining the built-in functions of the Apache server and IPCop's own scripts it is possible for the developers to accomplish very advanced tasks with minimal effort. This stability and ease of use is then transparently transferred to the user. Completely unaware that Apache is part of the system doing the work, the user can go about configuring the firewall with only the knowledge required to browse the Web. Since this is fast becoming an essential skill and has joined reading and writing as one of the skill-sets taught in school classrooms, it makes IPCop extremely approachable. The use of approachable technology such as this is one of the many ways in which IPCop strives to achieve its goals.

Equally in networks with no full time IT staff and those with staff for whom IPCop constitutes only a small allocation of time, ease of use becomes vital. Most IPCop users don't want to know about the inner workings of creating and maintaining session state rules for packet filtering. IPCop aims to make this sort of knowledge unnecessary. The front end allows us to quickly configure the basic and advanced features of our firewall without knowing the in-depth details of underlying systems. With this ease of use there are also some powerful configuration options, which allow us to set up configurations that are quite advanced and would be much more difficult to set up using the tools IPCop is built on. **Virtual Private Networking** and **Quality of Service** controls are excellent examples of this—individually, the packages providing these services have a very steep learning curve, but when incorporated into IPCop, they are relatively easy to configure.

The Gap IPCop Fills

There are a variety of different levels of firewall available. At one end of the spectrum, there are enterprise systems such as Check Point and ISA, which perform all kinds of powerful functions and can control the traffic for networks of vastly varying sizes and topologies. At the other end of the spectrum, we have personal firewalls running on host machines such as Agnitum, ZoneAlarm, and the built-in firewall in Windows XP Service Pack 2, which protect a single machine. There are also many home routers that provide basic firewall functionality. This leaves us with the question as to which of these roles IPCop is appropriate for, and whether it suits our needs.

IPCop is best suited, as we discussed earlier, to the SOHO network. If our network is relatively small with a single Internet connection, such as a home network or small business, or we have a couple of sites with separate internet connections that require linking together in a medium-sized business then we can certainly benefit from using IPCop to handle these connections. Another important aspect of IPCop is cost. Since IPCop itself is free of charge our only expenses for the firewall are the cost of the hardware (which is usually a low-specification machine) and the cost of administering the machine (which is relatively low due to the easy-to-use interface). For smaller networks this is highly attractive.

Systems such as ISA server and checkpoint are extremely expensive and require a great deal of background knowledge to configure and secure properly. Compare this to IPCop, which functions as a very well-secured router and firewall almost by default. Larger enterprise systems also have much higher system requirements and are usually overkill for smaller networks. The expense and time it takes to set these up is unlikely to provide a good return on investment for networks outside the larger enterprise. IPCop also benefits from simplicity that is not available when using a general purpose OS such as Windows or even a Linux distribution with all the unnecessary services they usually come with. IPCop has a specific role, so many services and other applications can be removed such that you are left with a specialized system.

At the other end of the spectrum, there are personal firewalls such as those provided by Agnitum, ZoneAlarm, et al. Commonly within SOHO offices Windows Internet Connection Sharing (or a cheap router) is used to fulfill the role frequently occupied by IPCop.

These firewalls generally provide basic features and don't allow us to create VPNs or to protect multiple machines from a single centralized device. When you consider the features such as the ability to create a DMZ, the Intrusion Detection System and the network services provided by IPCop you can see that simple host-based systems may not be adequate for us and something with the power of IPCop as well as its ease of use becomes a compelling option.

The most common use of IPCop, at the moment, is among people who have some firewall and Linux knowledge but don't want to spend time setting up a firewall from scratch. This is by no means the only use for IPCop. No real Linux or firewall experience is necessary and the purpose of this book is to walk through IPCop in an easy-to-follow way, which enables a user with the most basic computer knowledge to get up and running with a simple firewall to protect their network.

Features of IPCop

Throughout this book we will be discussing version 1.4.10 of IPCop, which is the latest release at time of writing. As IPCop is continually being developed new features will be added and some of these features may change.

Web Interface

A lot of firewalls come with a cluttered, complex user front end that requires significant amount of training and experience to become familiar with. The ISA server interface, for instance, is famously unintuitive and often interfaces aren't designed in order to make common tasks simple and easy to accomplish.

Frequently, proprietary firewalls such as ISA server and BorderWare will rename common functions such as **port forwarding** and refer to them as something entirely different, not making life any easier even for an administrator with experience of firewalls, but no knowledge of the particular user interface in question. As an easy example of this, BorderWare refers to port forwarding as an **internal proxy**, ISA as **publishing**, and DrayTek's line of (reliable and full-featured, but somewhat tricky-to-configure) routers refer to it as a virtual server. These definitions in some instances have a reason (application-layer firewalls will proxy traffic, as we discovered earlier), but don't really make life easier, even if they have a justification!

We will take a close look at how to set up IPCop and therefore will spend a lot of time inside the interface. It is therefore extremely fortunate that the interface is quite easy to use and very intuitive. The IPCop developers have decided to use an interface based on a website built into the system with the consequence that for most people, the interface is a familiar environment as it is quite unlikely that anyone setting up a firewall has never used a website.

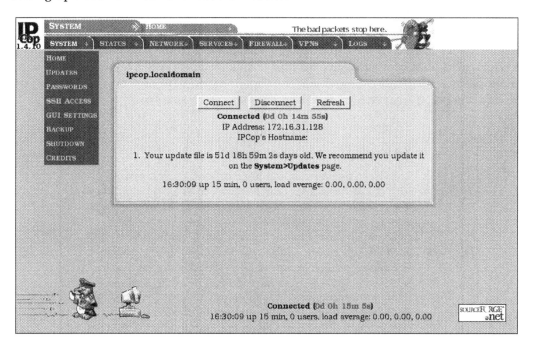

Merely using a website as the **Graphical User Interface** (**GUI**) is not enough. The interface still has to be set out so that it is easy to figure out and access all of the common functions. Most of the functions we will look at will consist of filling simple forms, which is an effective and easy-to-manage interface. IPCop isn't unique in using such an interface. Many devices such as SOHO cable routers made by Linksys, DrayTek, and D-Link have a similar setup, and many high-end products from Cisco appliances to HP Procurve switches do too, but few of these contain all of the features and the ease of use provided by IPCop.

Network Interfaces

IPCop provides up to four network interfaces, each of which is usually connected to a separate network. This is an adequate number for most IPCop deployments as it is rare to have many networks converging at one point in a small to medium sized network, but IPCop can accommodate connections to more networks than this through use of Virtual Private Network (VPN). The four networks available are given identifying colors for ease of administration.

The Green Network Interface

The Green network segment of an IPCop deployment represents the *internal* network, and is implicitly trusted. An IPCop firewall will automatically allow all connections *from* the Green segment *to* all other segments.

The Green segment is always an Ethernet Network Interface Card (NIC), and there is no support for any other device utilized in this capacity. A local network may be as simple as a small hub plugged into the Green interface, or may encompass several dozen switches, a layer two bridge to another site, or even a router.

Addressing on the Green Interface

The Green network should use a private address range (private address ranges can be found in RFC1918). Although it is possible to set this up with a publicly addressable address range, the default IPCop configuration is one in which NAT is used to expose only one IP address, and as such, using a public address range on the Green network segment would be pointless, as IPCop would treat it as if it were a private address range! Using IPCop as a routing firewall (rather than a firewall performing NAT, which is the default configuration) requires more advanced configuration and cannot be accomplished through the GUI.

Typically, a network approaching this complexity would choose to segment its network with one or more firewalls or routers built on IPCop, another free software package, or a commercial package, but with adequate knowledge of networking and several hardware platforms, one could build a complex, secure network topology using IPCop.

The Red Network Interface

Similar to the Green network interface, the Red network interface is always present. The Red network interface represents either the Internet or an untrusted network segment (in a larger topology).

The principle goal of the IPCop firewall is to protect the Green, Blue, and Orange segments and the networked hosts on them from traffic, users, and hosts on the Red segment. The Red network segment is typically well-firewalled and will not open a large number of ports into the internal network segments (if any at all). The default is none.

Addressing on the Red Interface

The Red segment will almost always use a public address range, assigned by your Internet Service Provider. It is possible (but less common) for Internet Service Providers to use private address ranges for large portions of their internal networks and to perform NAT at the border in between their network and the Internet-exposed backbone.

GPRS and 3G networks commonly do this, as do some cable ISPs. If in doubt, ask your ISP or check an existing machine or router connected to your ISP. The website www. dnsstuff.com can be used to **WHOIS** an IP address to check the registration, and if you're unsure as to whether an IP address is *private* or *public*, this can be an excellent way to check the ownership.

The Red network segment is the *only* network segment on which IPCop has support for hardware other than an Ethernet Network Interface Card. The Red segment may be an Ethernet network interface allocated statically or using DHCP, it may be a USB ADSL modem, an ISDN card, or even a dial-up, analog modem connected to the Public Switched Telephone Network.

Other hardware interfaces that IPCop will support on this interface include:

USB and PCI ADSL Modems

DSL is a technology that allows a broadband, high-speed internet or network signal to be sent over an existing copper phone line. This form of internet provision is extremely popular, particularly in countries with traditionally lower uptake of services like cable, as it requires no expensive digging up and rewiring of streets and premises with new wiring for cable or network infrastructure. One of the downsides of DSL is the comparatively short range of DSL signals, necessitating proximity to a telephone exchange, although this limit increases as technology advances.

IPCop will allow users with DSL services (both **SDSL** and **ADSL**) to attach certain brands of modem directly to the IPCop firewall. There are three principle ways to attach an IPCop firewall to a DSL line.

The first of these is to attach the IPCop host to an ADSL modem via Ethernet. Generally the most stable way, this has the disadvantage of being more difficult to set up. Modems that are full-fledged routers, such as the many routers based around Conexant chipsets, are generally designed to act as the NAT router in a network themselves. These devices have either one Ethernet port (which plugs into a switch or hub) or several Ethernet ports (and a small built-in switch), and hand out private addresses (frequently in the 10.0.0.0/8 range) to clients on the network themselves, acting as a firewall. Connecting an IPCop host to the rear of one of these routers without altering the default configuration is a bad idea, as you are performing Network Address Translation twice.

While NAT frequently breaks protocols when performed once, performing it twice is almost a guaranteed way to give you networking headaches. In addition to the routing issues caused by essentially having two networks between you and the Internet, it is very hard to achieve port forwarding through these routers for protocols such as BitTorrent, SIP, online gaming, or incoming services like SMTP mail, as each port forward must be configured twice. These routers must therefore be configured *not* to act as NAT gateways, but instead fallback to behaving like *normal* routers. Without more than one IP address this is impossible, leaving home users or businesses without a fixed pool of IP addresses from their ISP in a conundrum if they wish to use IPCop!

Some ADSL routers that are Ethernet-based, therefore, have a feature referred to as **PPP Half Bridge**. This feature allows the device plugged in via Ethernet (i.e. your IPCop firewall) to get the *public* IP address from your ISP, and disables the router from acting as a firewall or NAT gateway. When acting in this mode, an ADSL router takes the IP address allocated by the ISP during authentication, and gives it to the first device that requests a DHCP address via DHCP. This function should be documented in your ADSL manual.

The second way to configure ADSL is using a USB ADSL modem attached directly to the PC or firewall. While perhaps simplest (as it requires minimal knowledge of networking, and no complex cabling or hardware installation), these modems are the cheapest, least reliable, and have the poorest performance of all three methods.

The third way to configure ADSL is using internal ADSL or SDSL cards, occupying one PCI slot inside a firewall, PC, or server. This is perhaps the least common method of configuring ADSL.

IPCop supports all three, to an extent: Wherever possible, the authors strongly recommend the use of an Ethernet ADSL modem either configured as a router using a static set of addresses, or (if this isn't possible) using DHCP either natively or using a workaround like PPP Half Bridge. Here is a list of supported devices in IPCop:

- The Alcatel SpeedTouch series of USB ADSL modems
- ECI USB ADSL devices (including BT Voyager Modems, the Zoom 5510 ADSL modem, and several dozen other similar devices)
- BeWan USB/PCI ADSL modems (the ST series of USB modem, and the ST series of PCI modem)
- Conexant USB modems (including the Zoom 5510, DrayTek Vigor 318, and several others)
- Conexant PCI modems
- Amedyn ADSL modems (for which the HCL lists only the Zyxel 630-11, Asus AAM6000UG USB)
- The 3com 3CP4218 USB ADSL modem

ISDN Modems

Integrated Services Digital Network (ISDN) is a form of (slow) broadband internet access provision predating ADSL or Cable connections. ISDN is essentially a form of digital circuit telephone line. ISDN was frequently used before the widespread adoption of broadband via cable, DSL, and satellite, and still sees usage in some branch offices, for remote working, and in areas with no DSL, cable, or satellite availability.

IPCop has support for a large number of ISDN modems (the 1.4.10 HCL lists 34). The full list is available on the IPCop Wiki site (`http://www.ipcop.org/modules.php?op=modload&name=phpWiki&file=index&pagename=IPCopHCLv01`).

Analog (POTS) Modems

IPCop should support any hardware analog (dial-up) modem. Hardware devices are generally attached via a serial port or as an ISA card.

Newer modems using the PCI interface are frequently *software* based. This means that a certain proportion of the modem's work is performed on the CPU of the computer it is attached to, by software, rather than by the modem itself.

Without device drivers that perform this work, such modems will not work, and as there are typically no drivers for these devices written for the Linux operating system, they are generally viewed as *broken* in Linux. USB modems should also work in IPCop.

The IPCop HCL lists one PCI modem that works with IPCop, the *PCI Smartlink 5634PCV*.

Cable and Satellite Internet

Generally speaking, internet services via cable from providers in Europe and the USA provide Ethernet modems that will *just work* in IPCop as they provide a public, routable IP address via DHCP. Some cable providers, however, provide USB modems that are unlikely to work in IPCop. The same is true of satellite internet (that USB modems are unlikely to work in IPCop).

The Orange Network Interface

The *optional* Orange network interface is designed as a **DMZ** network (see `http://www.firewall.cx/dmz.php` for more information on DMZ firewalls). In military terminology, a DMZ (DeMiliatized Zone) is an area where military activity is not permitted, such as a frontier in between two distinct (and hostile) countries. In firewall terminology, then, the term *DMZ* takes on a similar meaning, as a network segment in between the internal network of an organization and an external network such as the Internet. In this segment, servers are protected from the Internet by firewalls, but segregated (as they have internet exposure) from internal clients that are in a more protected zone behind the front line.

It is into this untrusted but segregated network that an organization will generally put any service designed to face the outside world, such as a web server (which serves outside clients for website requests), or more commonly a mail server (to which outside servers connect in order to deliver mail via SMTP).

Addressing on the Orange Interface

The Orange network interface generally uses a private address range as NAT is performed by IPCop. As with the Green zone, a *routing* rather than *NATing* firewall requires advanced configuration.

For this reason, the DMZ is considered to be an untrusted network segment, second only to the Red network interface. Hosts on the Orange network segment *cannot* connect to the Green or Blue network segments — all traffic from the Orange network segment to these internal segments must be explicitly allowed via **DMZ pinholes**. Traffic from the Red network segment to the Orange segment is allowed via port forwarding.

Clients on the Orange network should *not*, however, use the IPCop firewall as a DNS or DHCP server. There are valid security reasons for this—additional exposure to services on the IPCop host for this segment, apart from being harder to configure, increases the exposure of the IPCop host to attack from the Orange zone, decreasing the ability to provide secure services for clients in the Green zone.

The Blue Network Interfaces

The *optional* Blue network interface is a comparatively recent addition to IPCop, arriving with the 1.4 release series. This network is designed specifically for a separate wireless segment. Hosts on the Blue segment cannot get to the Green network other than through specific *pinholes* in a similar manner to the Orange network.

Addressing on the Blue Network Segment

The Blue network will almost always use a private address range.

IPCop also allows for the capability to connect to the Green zone via a Virtual Private Network, allowing clients to fully access resources on this network segment.

The Blue segment does not necessarily have to be a wireless segment—as the Blue segment is simply another network segment, and the wireless connection of hosts is transparent to IPCop, there is absolutely nothing stopping you from using the Blue segment as another subnet on your network if you are outgrowing the number of hosts available to you in your Green zone.

Using the Blue zone in this manner would also be a good way to separate hosts with distinct usage of the network, such as a subnet of workstations used by a particular group of staff, in public areas, or on a factory floor. The Blue zone might even be used as the default zone for a network in which the administrator did not want the hosts on the network to automatically have access to every resource on the network, as the Green zone does.

In such a topology, the IT staff might be allocated the Green zone in order to access network resources, while workstations might be kept in the Blue zone, with specific access to areas of the network they required.

Simple Administration and Monitoring

As a device that aims to be easy to use, it would not be of much use to the user if he or she had to reinstall each time a new version came out. It would also be extremely beneficial if the user didn't have to log in to the Linux console on the machine at any time. The IPCop developers obviously agree with this and therefore have a built in a simple upgrade system. This can be managed entirely from the web interface. If, however, the user did want to log in to the Linux console and make changes this could be done quite simply by using a keyboard/monitor attached to the machine or by using SSH from a computer on the local network (Green interface). SSH, for added security, is disabled by default and would have to be enabled before it could be used.

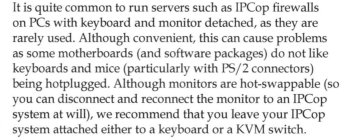

Local Console

It is quite common to run servers such as IPCop firewalls on PCs with keyboard and monitor detached, as they are rarely used. Although convenient, this can cause problems as some motherboards (and software packages) do not like keyboards and mice (particularly with PS/2 connectors) being hotplugged. Although monitors are hot-swappable (so you can disconnect and reconnect the monitor to an IPCop system at will), we recommend that you leave your IPCop system attached either to a keyboard or a KVM switch.

Another side effect of leaving the keyboard detached is that the BIOS in many computers will *halt* on startup and await a keypress if it does not see a keyboard attached. For computers that do not have keyboards attached, this behavior can (and really should) usually be disabled in the BIOS configuration.

You can also back up and restore your configuration from this same interface, which ensures that all common administration tasks for the firewall can be managed very easily and more importantly without any knowledge about Linux or the bash shell.

With the status provided on the web interface we can see exactly how the system is doing. For example we can see which services are currently running on the firewall, memory and disk usage, as well as traffic graphs, if we have an interest in this.

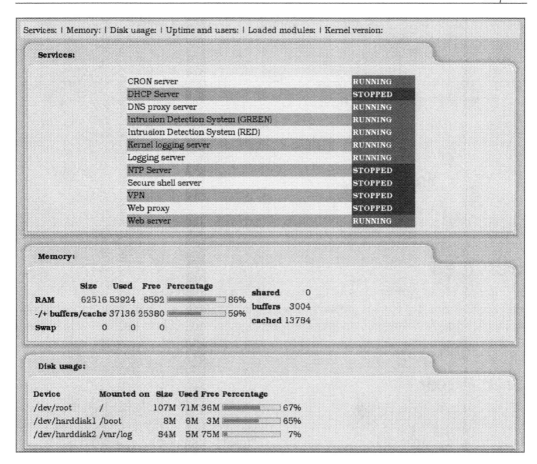

Again these features show the power of the web-based interface and why this particular interface was chosen. We can also quickly see important system information without logging in to the system with an interactive shell.

Logs can also be viewed using the web-based log viewer, which means you can keep an eye on the system quite easily with absolutely no need to log directly into the system. IPCop also has the ability to export these logs to a remote Syslog server for simplified management and log aggregation, especially if you have a few devices to monitor.

Modem Settings

As many home users are using ISDN or ADSL modems for dial-up (including USB/ADSL modems), it's important that IPCop supports them. A variety of common modems are supported and IPCop has the functionality to have additional drivers loaded for modems it does not support by default, and the configuration options for these are fairly flexible. It's not very common for firewalls to support modems and drivers for them in this manner; this is one of the most unique features of IPCop and why it fits so well in the SOHO network.

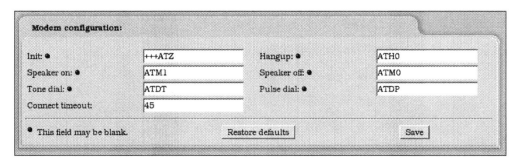

Services

IPCop provides a variety of essential services for a small network. It's not strictly firewall best practice to provide such services on the same box that is supposed to be a network protection mechanism, but economy comes into play on smaller networks and it's very useful to have all the basic network services provided by a single machine.

Web Proxy

IPCop can be used as a proxy as well as a firewall. You can easily manage the cache and configure the proxy on the Green interface. The benefit of the defined interfaces becomes quite apparent here as it means a simple checkbox click is all that is required to set up proxying on IPCop.

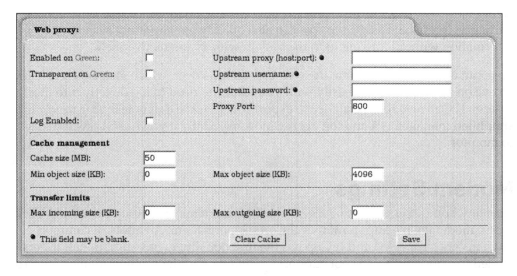

DHCP

As a network grows, allocating network configuration to clients manually becomes extremely difficult, and it's fairly important to be able to automate this, as well as manage the use of the network addresses you use. The **Dynamic Host Configuration Protocol** (**DHCP**) configuration in IPCop makes it easy for you to provide DHCP services to the clients on the Green interface if you're unsure of how to do this. Doing this via DHCP simplifies client-side configuration, meaning that most machines will connect to the network and have internet access automatically without any configuration required on the host.

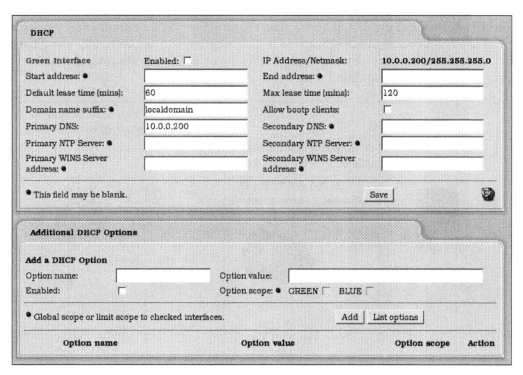

Dynamic DNS

Generally speaking, internet connections for SOHO users will have a **Fully Qualified Domain Name** (**FQDN**) something like 31-34-43-10.some ISP.net. The FQDN of a computer on the Internet can be used to make connections to it—so a connection made to Google, for instance, goes to www.google.com. For a home user, your FQDN is not a domain name like **google.com**, but instead a domain name used by your ISP to identify what ISP you're coming from and which client you are on your network, and generally make things a bit more understandable for humans.

While this makes sense for an ISP managing its clients, it makes connecting remotely to a network that has internet connectivity provided like this difficult. Even if you could memorize and hand out your ISP's allocated domain name, it would still not be a solution if you want people to be able to access services you host, as the IP address, and therefore the FQDN of your firewall or router would change from time to time.

Therefore, many networks use **Dynamic DNS**. Using a dynamic DNS system, a small piece of software running on a firewall or client attached to the Internet will update a server on the Internet (a dynamic DNS server) with your IP address, and redirect a fixed hostname (such as yourname.dynamicdnsprovider.com) to whatever your IP address is at present. If you connect to an IPSec VPN, or another service such as HTTP, VNC, or a terminal service, or if clients connect to you remotely using these protocols, the connections can be made to this dynamic DNS hostname, and will seamlessly go to the IP updated with the dynamic DNS server.

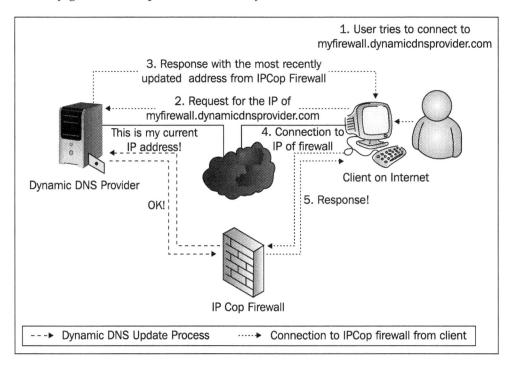

Since these services require constantly updating a server with your current IP address in order to keep the DNS working, use of dynamic DNS requires a computer or other device running software constantly talking to a Dynamic DNS Provider.

Dynamic DNS is a feature not commonly found in larger firewall products and certainly isn't common in most low-end home routers.

Settings

Dynamic DNS provider(s) will receive an IP address for this IPCop from:

⊙ The classical RED IP used by IPCop during connection

○ Guess the real public IP with help of an external server ●

☐ Minimize updates: before an update, compares the dns IP for hostname "[host.]domain" against RED IP.

● Do not use this option with Dial on Demand! Mainly used if your IPCop is behind
a router. Your RED IP must be inside one of the three reserved network numbers   [Save]
e.g. 10/8, 172.16/12, 192.168/16

Add a host:

Service:	dyndns.org ▾	Hostname: ●	
Behind a proxy:	☐	Domain:	
Enable wildcards:	☐	User Name:	
		Password:	
Enabled:	☑	Again:	

● To use no-ip in group mode, prefix hostname with **noipg-**   [Add]

Current hosts:

Service	Hostname	Domain	Proxy	Wildcards	Action

Time Server

Hosts on the network commonly need to be configured to keep the same time, whether this is because of authentication mechanisms such as Kerberos or merely for convenience. IPCop provides the **Network Time Protocol** (**NTP**) service, which can be used to keep all clients on the network synchronized.

Using NTP, the IPCop server connects to an NTP timeserver on the Internet, from which it ascertains the correct time. It then keeps this internally using the computer's clock, and acts as an NTP server for clients within the network. By regularly updating from an upstream NTP server, the IPCop box can ensure that the time is kept to a reasonable degree of accuracy.

By updating from a local source, rather than having every local client update from an external time source, you keep clients accurate to each other (so even if the time isn't strictly accurate, you know all of your local clients keep approximately the same time, important for things like log auditing and Kerberos). Most importantly, it also reduces the load on NTP servers, which are providing you with a free service!

Information on how to configure client operating systems to talk to an NTP server can be found here:

- Windows: `http://www.boulder.nist.gov/timefreq/service/pdf/win2000xp.pdf`

- Linux: `http://Linuxreviews.org/howtos/ntp/`

- OS X: Select **System Preferences**, and **Use Network Time**

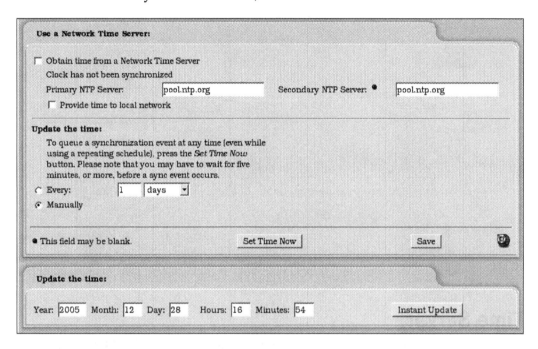

Advanced Network Services

Traffic shaping and intrusion detection are quite advanced network services that we wouldn't expect to see in most SOHO devices. IPCop not only provides these, but also makes them very easy to manage, and as we look at configuring IPCop, we will see exactly how easily these quite complicated systems can be maintained.

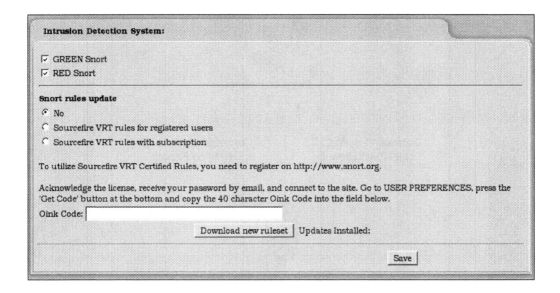

Port Forwarding

This is a feature that is quite common in a firewall from SOHO to large enterprises. The benefits of IPCop here are twofold. Firstly, we don't have any limitations on the number of forwardings we can add and secondly it is very easy to set up. With some SOHO devices not only do we have limitations on the number of ports we can forward, but we also often find very complicated configurations surrounding it. Enterprise systems are complicated by nature and in this particular feature the complication is exacerbated.

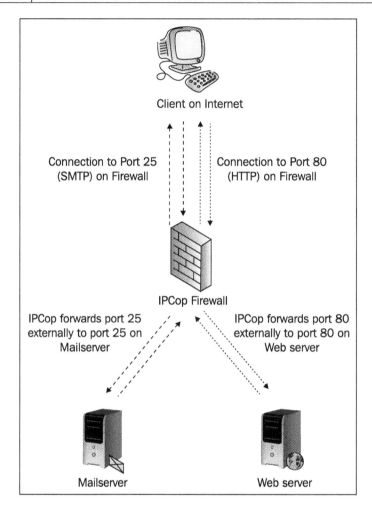

As we can see, the IPCop firewall appears to the client to be both a mail server *and* a web server, but connections to ports 25 and 80 in this example configuration are in fact forwarded to the servers configured in the port forwarding menu. These servers in an IPCop configuration would probably be in the Orange zone.

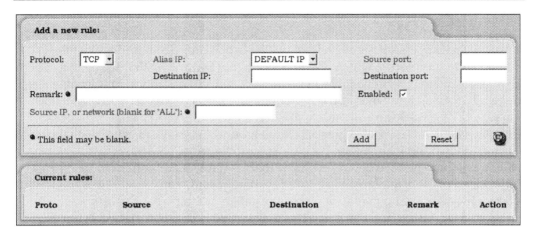

Virtual Private Networking

This gives you the ability to join to more networks across the Internet with a (virtually) private link. This is one of the main features of IPCop, which means it can also be used in a medium-sized business and not just a SOHO network. The ins and outs of the IPCop VPN implementation are thoroughly discussed in a later chapter.

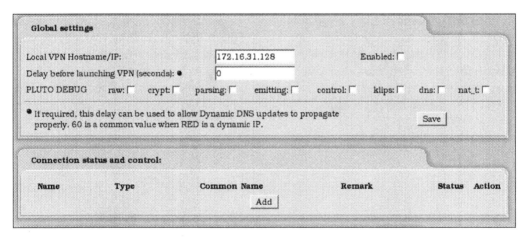

ProPolice Stack Protection

IPCop has been built to use ProPolice, which is a mechanism used to protect the services running on the firewall from being attacked via the Internet. The stack protection provided by ProPolice is a fairly effective mechanism to prevent a particular kind of vulnerability common in network services.

Why IPCop?

When evaluating IPCop for use within our environment, we should look at the functionality it provides, which is evident from the feature list that we have just seen. Then, we need to determine if it will be the most effective solution for our network. Generally for a small to medium sized network IPCop is extremely beneficial and can simplify network administration greatly. However, for very large networks where we have a variety of segments all interconnecting with varying mechanisms we may find IPCop inadequate. It's important to figure out how exactly our network will fit together and then choose IPCop if there is a role it could fit in to. For the SOHO network this may be a very simple topology and may require little thought. In a larger network IPCop may have scope for deployment in specific roles within the infrastructure, for example as the gateway device of key remote networks, such as branch offices.

Summary

In this chapter we had a look at the feature-set available in IPCop. We have an idea of what exactly IPCop can do, and combined with the knowledge of the previous chapter, we know how it stacks up as a firewall. We now also have an idea of the situations in which IPCop could be useful and what we will need to understand in order to use it. Some of the screenshots may look a little bit complicated at this point, if we are new to any of the topics. As we go through these functions, everything will be explained so that we understand each option fully and know whether we need to configure that particular area and how exactly we would want it set up. For those more familiar with the technologies this may have served to give an overview of how some of the features work within IPCop.

3
Deploying IPCop and Designing a Network

Now that we understand what IPCop is capable of as a firewall unconnected to any other system, we need to start considering how it does connect to them, and what are the implications for us. As you must now be realizing, the scope for deploying IPCop is quite varied, and especially in conjunction with a knowledge of Linux and the flexibility of open-source software, the number of possible permutations of even one IPCop box are fairly limitless! That said, there is a core of functionality used by the majority of networks, and among all of those permutations, there are a few core network layouts that will probably be common among the majority of IPCop deployments.

What we will try to do here, therefore, is outline a few common methods of deploying IPCop and the motivation behind these topologies, depending on which IPCop components we want to deploy.

Trust Relationships between the Interfaces

As we now understand, the four types of network interface—Green, Red, Blue, and Orange—supported by IPCop have differing levels of trust associated with them. Here is a simple table outlining what traffic is allowed to go to and from which interfaces. This table, and the knowledge contained within it, should form the basis of our planning when considering how many interfaces to use and what to use them for. This is basically the Traffic Flow diagram from the IPCop administrative guide (http://www.ipcop.org/1.4.0/en/admin/html/section-firewall.html).

Interface From	Interface To	Status	How To Access
Red	Firewall	CLOSED	External Access
Red	Orange	CLOSED	Port Forwarding
Red	Blue	CLOSED	Port Forwarding / VPN
Red	Green	CLOSED	Port Forwarding / VPN
Orange	Firewall	CLOSED	
Orange	Red	OPEN	
Orange	Blue	CLOSED	DMZ Pinholes
Orange	Green	CLOSED	DMZ Pinholes
Blue	Firewall	CLOSED	Blue Access
Blue	Red	CLOSED	Blue Access
Blue	Orange	CLOSED	Blue Access
Blue	Green	CLOSED	DMZ Pinholes / VPN
Green	Firewall	OPEN	
Green	Red	OPEN	
Green	Orange	OPEN	
Green	Blue	OPEN	

In visualizing the way in which traffic goes through the IPCop firewall, we can see it as a sort of giant junction with a traffic cop (literally, an IP Cop—hence the name!) in the middle of it. When a car (in network parlance, a packet of data) reaches the crossroads, the cop decides in which direction the packet should go (based on the routing tables IPCop uses), and pushes it in the appropriate direction.

In the case of a Green client accessing the Internet, we can see from the previous table that this access is OPEN, so the cop allows the traffic through. In other instances, however, this might not be the case. If a Blue client tries to access a client on the Green segment, for instance, the cop might allow the traffic through if it comes over a VPN or through DMZ pinholes—but if a client on the Blue segment has neither of these things explicitly allowing the traffic, it is stopped. The car is pulled over, the occupants victims of some virtual time in the cells!

Note that (generally) when we illustrate IPCop Configurations, the Red interface is uppermost (North), the Orange interface is to the left (West), the Blue interface is to the right (East), and the Green interface is to the bottom (South). With all four interfaces, this appears like this:

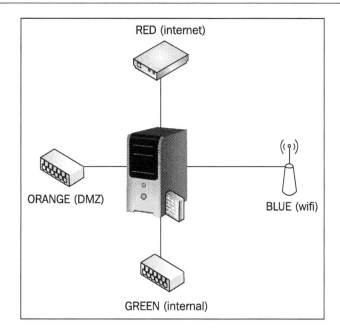

Altering IPCop Functionality

As with many aspects of the behavior of the IPCop firewall, it is possible to alter the behavior of the firewalling rules in order to customize IPCop to meet a topology un-catered for by the default rules. Within the context of the firewall rules, IPCop has had a file since the 1.4-series release that allows users to specifically add their own firewall rules (`/etc/rc.d/rc.firewall.local`). Since version 1.3, there have been iptables chains, *CUSTOMINPUT*, *CUSTOMFORWARD*, etc., allowing iptables rules to be added manually.

Specifically using iptables is out of our scope here, but we recommend that interested readers read:

The Linux iptables HOWTO at `http://www.linuxguruz.com/iptables/howto/`

Topology One: NAT Firewall

Our first topology exists as a drop-in replacement for the many NAT firewalls that exist in the market. In small offices and homes, solutions such as the embedded NAT firewalls sold by D-Link, Linksys, and friends are frequently deployed in order to provide small networks with cost-effective Internet access. Solutions such as **Internet Connection Sharing** (see `http://www.microsoft.com/windowsxp/using/networking/learnmore/default.mspx` for more information on Internet

Connection Sharing from Microsoft), a combined NAT firewall, DNS Proxy, and DHCP Server, built into client editions of Windows since Windows 98, are also frequently used in order to allow one PC with a modem or network interface to act as a network gateway for other clients. For our purposes here, we will consider **ICS**, as such a topology with ICS is effectively a superset of the work required to replace a router such as a Linksys or NETGEAR model as mentioned previously Our migration from one of these routers to IPCop would be identical save for the decommissioning of the ICS software on the client—if we remove the router, this is unnecessary and the router can be left configured as-is (and/or kept as a backup, or reused elsewhere) (See `http://www.annoyances.org/exec/show/ics` for more information on implementing (and consequently, decommissioning) ICS on different Windows versions).

Such a topology with ICS might look like this:

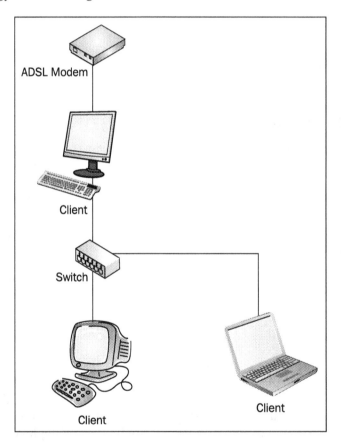

Such solutions, while cheap and convenient, are often not scalable or reliable, and provide poor security. They open workstations up to unnecessary security risks, provide limited throughput, and are often unreliable, requiring frequent reboots and locking up.

As with software firewalls, a network firewall is designed as a barrier in between your workstations and the Internet. By connecting one of your workstations directly to the Internet and using a solution like ICS, although you reduce the resources required to share the internet connection, you expose that workstation to unnecessary risk. There is also an obligation for that PC to be on all the time — compared to a low-end PC with no unnecessary components and a low-power PSU running IPCop, this may be noisier, and have more power consumption.

IPCop offers a cost-effective replacement in such situations, providing small businesses and home users with a powerful firewall without the need for over-complexity, and adding other features not present in embedded solutions or ICS, such as a customizable DHCP Server, Intrusion Detection, a Proxy Server, and so on.

With IPCop acting as a replacement in this situation, the replacement network might look like this:

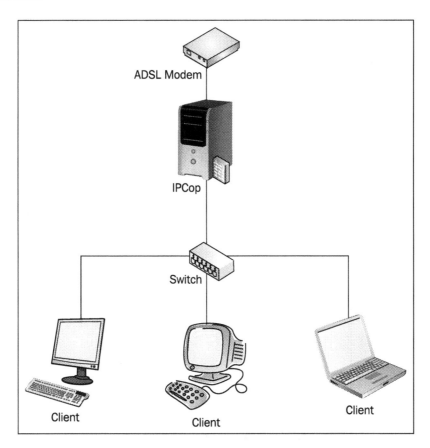

Such a topology ensures that firewalling is done before data gets to clients, using a package designed to act as a network firewall, greatly increasing the quality of service to clients as well as the security that their network offers. In this situation, the components of IPCop in use would be:

- Green/Red zones
- DHCP Server
- DNS Server

In such a situation, a network administrator or consultant might also choose to enable any of the following pieces of functionality in order to enhance the services provided to the network:

- Intrusion Detection
- IPSec in order to allow remote work or remote support
- Port Forwarding in order to allow remote access to VNC or Terminal Services/Remote Desktop for a simplified model of remote access for remote support (more convenient than IPSec although inherently more insecure)

Decommissioning of ICS in such a situation is quite simple—we would merely disable the ICS functionality, as depicted in the following screenshot (taken from the network connections property of the external, internet-facing ICS network interface).

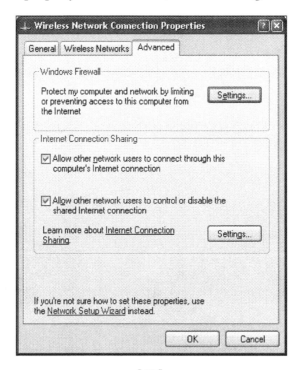

Removing ICS is as simple as deselecting the **Allow other network users to connect through this computer's Internet connection** option. After we have done this, we should hit **OK**, reboot if asked to, and then we are free to disable and/or remove the external interface on the workstation (disable if we wish to leave a second network card in the machine or if it has two onboard cards, or remove if we are using an external modem or other piece of hardware we intend to remove or install in our IPCop host).

IPCop's Intrusion Detection System

The Intrusion Detection feature is a powerful component of IPCop, which is easy to enable and use. Although precise analysis of the log files that IPCop's IDS generates requires considerable skill and experience, it is simple to turn on and unless there are specific space requirements for the IPCop firewall (i.e. it is running on a device with a very small hard disk or compact flash card, or with inadequate CPU/memory to perform analysis), there is no compelling reason not to enable the IDS system.

Firewall rules for this topology are simple; as the Green segment is automatically allowed to access resources on the Red interface, there is no topology-specific setup required in order to set this up.

Another substantial benefit in deploying IPCop for such a small office situation is that in the event that the business is required to grow, the solution that it has is scalable. Such a business running a handful of Windows workstations in a workgroup may decide that a workgroup is insufficient for its needs and that it requires centralized management, file storage, and configuration.

IPCop, even in a pre-upgrade scenario like this, is advantageous simply because it provides a built-in, open upgrade path. There is no hardware or software upgrade required to move from simple NAT and DHCP to a network with several network segments, port forwarding, and a proxy server. If the Server already has several network cards (and with the price of these nowadays, there's no reason for it not to, if an expansion is anticipated), this can even be done with little or no noticeable interruption in service to existing clients.

Topology Two: NAT Firewall with DMZ

In a small office situation with a growing company, the need for incoming email might force the activation of the Orange zone, and the deployment and installation of a mail server in this segment.

Such a company might choose to keep its Desktop and Internal Server infrastructure within the Green network segment and put their its server in the DMZ on a switch/hub, or simply attached to the Orange interface of the IPCop host using a crossover cable. As such systems are exposed to the Internet, this segmentation provides a considerable advantage by providing a 'stop line' past which it would be harder for an intruder to escalate his or her access to the network.

DMZ and External Network Segment Infrastructure

Although it's often extremely convenient to attach a DMZ server or external router to the firewall (or another router) using crossover cables, using a hub or switch can often pay dividends—inevitably, when you might actually need a switch or hub in this role may be while troubleshooting connectivity issues associated with these systems, and in such scenarios you may not be able to find and install a hub/switch in adequate time, or may not want to interrupt any connectivity that is still remaining.

Using hubs and switches also plans for future expansion, and enables you to add another system with even less effort. Small switches with half a dozen ports really aren't expensive, either!

Microsoft's Exchange mail server has for some time supported such a configuration through the use of the 'front end' and 'back end' exchange roles (although these roles will be deprecated with future Exchange releases). With a different network configuration however, such as Linux clients using a management system such as Novell's eDirectory or RedHat's Directory Server (RHDS), or a filtering appliance, a similar system with externally-facing SMTP servers (perhaps running the open-source MTA exim) would be equally beneficial.

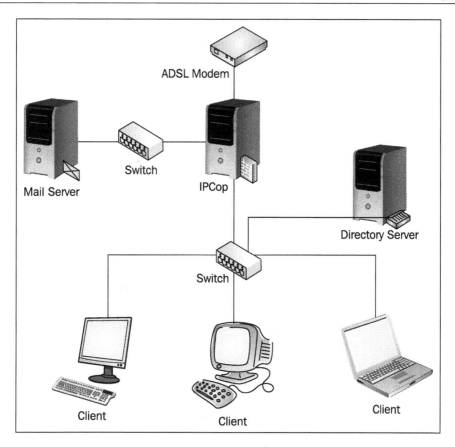

In this topology, Clients are freely able to connect to the mail server (whether via POP, IMAP, RPC, or RPC over HTTP). In order for a mail server that exists as part of the network domain to authenticate to the directory server, we would also need to open the appropriate ports (contingent upon the directory provider) to the directory server using the DMZ Pinholes feature.

Firewalling Active Directory Domain Controllers

Information on specifically which ports Active Directory needs to replicate (i.e. in between domain controllers, if a mail host and the directory server were domain controllers) is available at `http://www.microsoft.com/technet/prodtechnol/windows2000serv/technologies/activedirectory/deploy/confeat/adrepfir.mspx`

Although in such a scenario the security benefit to a DMZ would be limited as the compromise of the mail host would mean the compromise of a domain controller, there would still be a slight security benefit—running a domain controller in an internet-facing role, however, is not recommended!

Ports required by Clients or Servers talking to a domain controller can be found in the following article, which details the ports required to configure the Windows firewall on a Windows 2003 system:

`http://support.microsoft.com/default.aspx?scid=kb;en-us;555381&sd=rss&spid=3198`

We also have a Port Forwarding rule set up from the external IP address of the IPCop firewall to port 25 on the mail server. This allows external mail servers to connect to the mail server in order to deliver email.

In this topology, a compromise of the mail server (which in the Green segment could compromise the entire network segment) is controlled, as there is some level of protection provided by the firewall.

In such a topology, we use the following capabilities of the IPCop Firewall:

- Red, Orange, Green zones
- DMZ Pinholes
- DHCP Server
- DNS Server
- Port Forwarding to Orange segment

We might also choose to employ any of the following elements of functionality:

- Intrusion Detection System
- Port Forwarding to web server on the mail server (for external access of IMAP or Exchange mailboxes via a webmail solution such as Horde, SquirrelMail, or Outlook Web Access)

- Proxy Server (for desktop Internet access)

- IPSec for remote access to Servers in the Green and Orange segment or for external support

- Back-end mail server with mailboxes in the Green zone, using the Server in the Orange zone as a relay, performing anti-spam and anti-virus scanning/filtering

Topology Three: NAT Firewall with DMZ and Wireless

In a larger organization, or if the network above grew, we might choose to expand our network topology using one or more IPCop firewalls. Very large networks are out of the scope of this book alone, as they require aggregated knowledge and experience that a networking/IT professional will need to glean from multiple sources.

The IPCop Mailing List

The IPCop user mailing list is a very good source of information on extending IPCop and deploying it in more advanced roles. It is worth subscribing to and perusing for those who have more than a passing interest in IPCop. The archives for this mailing list can be found at `https://sourceforge.net/mailarchive/forum.php?forum_id=4957` and there is a subscription page at `http://lists.sourceforge.net/lists/listinfo/ipcop-user`.

Several IPCop firewalls might be used by such an individual in order to separate several sites, or in order to further segregate one or more DMZs with physically distinct firewalls.

It is also worth considering that IPCop is designed primarily for networks in which it is the only network firewall, in the Small and Medium Business, and Home/Home Office market. Although it is possible to set IPCop up in larger deployments, this is fairly rare, and there are other packages that are arguably more suited to such deployments. In such circumstances, the constraints of IPCop's network segmentation begin to be more burdensome than they are convenient, and the amount of work required to tailor IPCop to meet an organization's needs may exceed the work it would take to manually set up another firewall package to suit the same topology.

In this example, we will consider the broadest scope in which one IPCop box could be deployed, using all four network interfaces to protect a network with an internal (Green) network, an Internet or WAN connection (Red), a DMZ containing more than one Server (Orange), and a wireless segment (Blue) with an IPSec VPN system.

In such a situation, we would almost certainly choose to deploy all of the higher-end features that IPCop contains, such as the Proxy Server and the Intrusion Detection System.

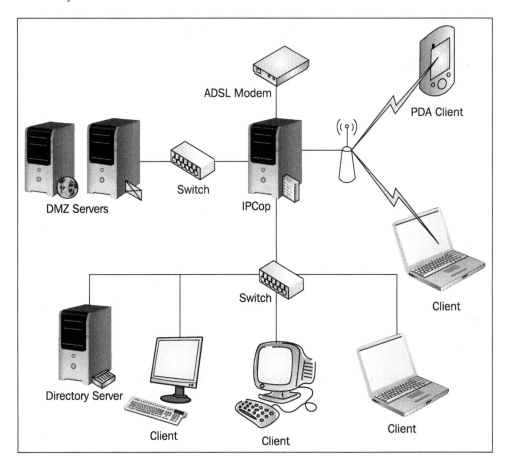

In this situation, the services we are providing for individual network interfaces are as follows:

On the Red Interface, in addition to the default firewalling policy, we are invoking the Port Forwarding feature to allow connections to the mail server on port 25 in the DMZ, and also to port 443 (HTTPS) on the mail server in order to allow connections to the business webmail system. We are also allowing incoming IPSec connections to the IPCop firewall in order to allow remote access to staff who work remotely and to provide remote connectivity for support purposes for the IT Staff and third-party software and hardware vendors.

On the Blue interface, we are providing connectivity via an IPSec VPN for clients in order that they can access services run from Servers internally on the Green segment and DMZ segment. Vendors and visitors are allowed access to the Green segment through use of WPA in pre-shared key mode configured on the wireless access point.

WPA and WEP

WPA was designed to introduce some features of a more advanced wireless standard designed to entirely supplant WEP, but before this standard was ready. The insecurity of the WEP system for securing 802.11 wireless LANs is well-documented, and WPA most notably employs the TKIP protocol (in addition to other changes) to constantly change the encryption key used to encrypt data transmitted over the air. Using TKIP, instead of one constantly used key, greatly reduces the severity of the encryption being broken (as in effect, it is only broken for a short timeframe), although it does mean that the Pre-Shared Key, used to generate these encryption keys, must be strong, and closely guarded.

WPA-RADIUS or WPA-Enterprise employs the use of a RADIUS server. RADIUS, which is often used to authenticate users to switches or systems for Internet Service provision, allows the access point to force client computers to authenticate to the RADIUS Server using a username and password or cryptographic certificate, before they are allowed to fully associate with the wireless access point. Utilization of a RADIUS server in this way is significantly more secure than WPA-PSK, both because the insecurity of the Pre-Shared Key is eliminated (each client has their own certificate or username/password, and these can be individually locked out or distributed) and also because a unique encrypted tunnel is created for each client, causing the wireless network to behave more, logically, like a switch than a hub (through the use of encryption).

WPA2, which eliminates some of the cryptographic weaknesses of WPA and TKIP, is stronger still, and uses the AES encryption standard for maximum data security.

Microsoft TechNet has excellent guides on implementing WPA-RADIUS using its RADIUS server (IAS, the Internet Authentication Service) available online via Microsoft TechNet, at the following URLs: Securing Wireless LANs with Certificate Services: `http://www.microsoft.com/ technet/security/prodtech/windowsserver2003/ pkiwire/swlan.mspx?mfr=true`

Securing Wireless LANs with PEAP and passwords: `http://www.microsoft.com/technet/security/ topics/cryptographyetc/peap_0.mspx`

WPA-PSK with solely an access point prevents access to the wireless segment and the Internet by unauthorized users, and is an adequate solution for most small and medium networks; use of a newer, WPA2-PSK-capable access point increases this security more for those without an access point or network infrastructure implementing RADIUS or Certificate Services.

The firewalling policy and IPSec system ensures that visitors/vendors only have access to the Red zone (the Internet), and not to any of the resources on the network.

On the Orange interface, our pinholes allow the DMZ servers to connect to a directory server and Kerberos domain controller in the Green segment in order to authenticate users logging onto them via the company directory system. This ensures that the policy and configuration for these Servers is managed centrally, and that there are logs stored centrally for them, but the damage that could be caused by a compromise of these externally-facing services is greatly minimized, ensuring business security and regulatory compliance.

On the Green interface, we allow connectivity to all interfaces, as workstations and Servers within the Green segment are managed service workstations on which users do not have the necessary level of access to cause damage to the resources to which they have access.

In such a situation, we are making use of the following IPCop features:

- Red, Orange, Green, Blue zones
- DMZ Pinholes
- DHCP Server

- DNS Server
- Port Forwarding to Orange segment
- IPSec for remote access to Green, Orange, Blue segments
- IPSec for access to internal resources by Blue users
- Intrusion Detection System
- Port Forwarding to web server on the Mail server externally
- Proxy Server (for desktop Internet access)

In a larger organization, we may also choose to use IPSec in site-to-site mode in order to link this office with one or more branch or parent offices. In this role as in the role of a single network firewall, IPCop excels.

Planning Site-To-Site VPN Topologies

In addition to *local* services such as those illustrated previously with our IPCop deployment, we may also be using the IPSec software in IPCop to configure a 'site-to-site' VPN to a branch or parent office, business partner, support company, or second site. In such situations, topology planning can become important as a network grows.

It is important, if we have more than one site, to consider exactly how we configure our VPN tunnels in order to provide a balance of service and stability to our clients. In a situation in which two branch offices attached to a main office both contain fileservers synchronizing content with each other, for instance, it would make little or no sense to setup two VPN tunnels from the branch offices to the main office in a 'spoke' topology. The extra hop would, during file transfers, slow down internet connectivity at the main site, and make for slow transfers.

Conversely, if we have many smaller offices with minimal requirements for site-to-site traffic and a head office with a large internet connection, we may decide that the added control of having all network activity converging through a single spot is worthwhile for us. As a network increases, forming individual VPN tunnels from site to site in a 'mesh' configuration can become very complex and hard to manage— although unlikely as a deployment with IPCop, such a deployment of more than a dozen or so servers would be increasingly hard to flexibly administer without thinking about using a routing protocol such as RIP or OSPF to calculate our routing tables for us!

When taking your VPN design into consideration, take a moment to ascertain your goals in terms of redundancy and speed (is the extra burden of setting up VPNs from remote offices to each other worth the redundancy in case your main site goes down, for instance?). Work it out on paper, think about what traffic will be going over your VPNs, and pick the best design for you that will scale.

Summary

In this chapter we have provided a high-level overview of three scenarios in which IPCop may be deployed in roles that suit it, along with an analysis of the benefits and pitfalls of IPCop usage in these situations.

These three topologies will be used further on in the book as case studies for maintenance and deployment.

Topology one: A dual-homed firewall performing Network Address Translation for a few clients. This is an excellent drop-in replacement for a small SOHO router or Microsoft's Internet Connection firewall. It is more secure, more reliable, and more scalable than other solutions for similar situations.

This topology uses IPCop's NAT features, and can use Port Forwarding for external services access and the Intrusion Detection System for added network security.

Topology two: A DMZ firewall with a separate segment for externally facing services such as incoming mail. Typically used by a small or medium business who have outgrown a single-subnet network, this is a common stepping stone between a small network with an embedded device and a larger network with a commercial or medium to high-end firewall.

This topology uses IPCop's NAT features, as well as DMZ pinholes in order to allow Servers in the DMZ segment to access resources and authenticate to Servers in the Green zone. The Intrusion Detection system may be used for added security, and Port Forwarding is used in order to allow external (Red zone) access to the services running on hosts in the DMZ.

Topology three: A DMZ firewall with separate segments for externally facing services such as incoming mail and for wireless access. This is typically used by a small or medium business that has outgrown a single-subnet network. This is similar to the second topology with the addition of a third internal segment, the Blue zone, for wireless clients on a less trusted network.

This might be a common extension of topology two or a way to segment a larger network with two workstation segments.

This topology uses IPCop's NAT features, as well as DMZ pinholes in order to allow Servers in the DMZ segment to access resources and authenticate to Servers in the Green zone. The Intrusion Detection system may be used for added security, and Port Forwarding is used in order to allow external (Red zone) access to the services running on hosts in the DMZ. The IPSec server is used in order to allow hosts in the Blue zone to access resources in the Green and Orange zones.

This topology may also be used in order to segment or provide better security to a network without the use of wireless technology.

4
Installing IPCop

Now that we have covered some basic networking and firewalling principles and are aware of the features that IPCop allows us to leverage, we can look at how to install the firewall. IPCop can be installed in a variety of ways, but using a CDROM (sometimes with an accompanying floppy disk) is the simplest and most common method. Therefore, we shall look at this installation method with a fairly detailed walk-through and in later sections we shall talk about the options we have for more advanced installations, such as installing over a network and debugging the installation procedure.

Hardware Requirements

IPCop has very modest minimum hardware requirements and is designed to be used on common PC hardware. Our main issue generally isn't *"is this machine powerful enough for IPCop"* it is more a case of *"is this machine powerful enough to handle the bandwidth going through it"*.

The minimum system requirements for IPCop are:

- A **386**-based **PC** or better (which means you can use a very old PC as your firewall)
- **32MB** of **RAM**
- **200MB hard drive** (or compact flash drive)
- **One Network Interface Card** (**NIC**) for each interface (four maximum). Each card has a unique hardware or MAC address, it's worth noting these down at this point for use in identifying the cards later.
- Connection devices for the Red interface if it's not Ethernet

Other Hardware Considerations

Although as a result of the minimum requirements for IPCop it is very tempting to put it on an old workstation or out-of-date PC, it is worth taking a step back to consider how we use it. In a home environment or in a very small office, an old PC may provide the requisite level of reliability, but it might not if internet access is critical, and especially if we use more complex functionality in IPCop such as VPNs or complex firewall rules, which are harder to duplicate, the damage caused by a hardware failure may be critical, even if we have backups.

A slightly more reliable, newer host therefore may be worth considering. There are also considerations based on the environment the firewall will be in. In a home or small office environment in which the firewall may not be in a server room or comms cupboard, the noise of an older PSU, while minimal, may be annoying. The power usage by such a server may also be a consideration—removing some unnecessary components or downgrading the PSU to a newer, more efficient, lower wattage model may solve the noise and power problems.

Hardware setup is worth considering, too—the location of our server should be considered such that rewiring is not an issue and the box will not require relocation or be tripped over. As we have mentioned before, we should also enable certain settings in the BIOS, such as disabling the 'halt on error' function (so that our box does not freeze at a prompt if the keyboard is removed or a component is damaged, unless we want this to happen). Another common BIOS option is the 'resume on power' option—causing our server to automatically turn back on in the event of a power outage.

The Installation Procedure

Before we begin installing IPCop, we have to ensure that we are fully prepared and have all the necessary equipment. The following is a short checklist to ensure we have everything we need before we begin; anything specific to IPCop such as CD and floppy media will be detailed during the installation walk-through.

- Do we have a machine that will meet the minimum system requirements?
- Do we have enough resources in the machine to handle our projected bandwidth usage?
- Do we have all required NICs and their drivers, if necessary, and have we checked they are compatible with IPCop?
- Do we have all the required equipment surrounding the IPCop machine in place? Examples are cabling, switches and a client machine to test the configuration.
- Do we have a working Internet connection?

As soon as we are sure we have all the prerequisite hardware and connections available, we can begin the installation. We will have to download the IPCop installation ISO and burn it to a CD. The latest version can be found at the SourceForge project page for IPCop `http://sourceforge.net/project/showfiles.php?group_id=40604` The latest version, at time of writing, is 1.4.10: `http://prdownloads.sourceforge.net/ipcop/ipcop-install-1.4.10.i386.iso?download`

After downloading the ISO and burning it to a CD with your choice of CD burning package we can begin the install.

Installing using a floppy

If your IPCop machine doesn't boot from CD, you can find a floppy image on the CD in the `images` folder, for example `boot-1.4.0.img`, which can be copied to a floppy disk, using the `dd` command on Linux or by using `rawwritewin.exe` provided on the IPCop disk.

Now we can boot the machine with the IPCop disk inserted in the CD drive, and we should then be presented with the following screen:

```
ISOLINUX 2.11 2004-08-16  Copyright (C) 1994-2004 H. Peter Anvin

    Welcome to IPCop, Licensed under GNU GPL version 2.

    PLEASE BEWARE!  This installation process will kill all
    existing partitions on your PC or server. Please be aware
    of this before continuing this installation.


    ----- ALL YOUR EXISTING DATA WILL BE DESTROYED -----



    Press RETURN to boot IPCop default installation.

    Or, if you are having trouble you can try these options....
    Type:   nopcmcia to disable PCMCIA detection
            nousb to disable USB detection
            nousborpcmcia to disable both PCMCIA & USB detection
            dma to enable ide dma (SiS chipset workaround)

boot:
```

As you can see there is a very prominent message that installing IPCop will destroy all data on the system. What this means is that the first disk that IPCop comes across will be wiped, repartitioned, and formatted for the IPCop system to install. For the safety of our data, it is very important that we verify that there is only one disk in the system and we are sure there is nothing of value stored there. Once we are sure of this we can begin the installation without fear of data loss.

Pressing *enter* at this point will boot us into the installation system but we can also supply additional parameters to the kernel. If after pressing *enter* the system fails to boot properly we should restart the machine and try with one of the options above. We can generally use the `nopcmcia` option if our machine doesn't have PCMCIA (commonly found on laptops) and the same goes for USB. Many IPCop systems run on old hardware and USB is less common on this.

After we hit *enter* we will then be presented with the language selection screen. Assuming we would like an English IPCop system we can go with the default option, otherwise choose our language of preference. You can use the arrow keys to navigate the menu entries. We will then see the IPCop welcome message with instructions to hit cancel at any time to cause a reboot, in case we change our mind about the install.

Installation Media

The next stage of the installation process, as shown in the following figure, is the choice of installation media.

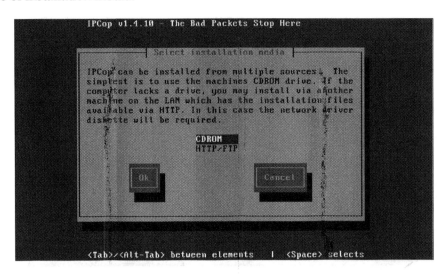

IPCop can be installed over FTP or HTTP for machines that do not have a CDROM drive. In this case, we would boot the machine off a floppy disk, and then have the host download that the content from the Internet normally is contained on the CDROM. Since we have a CDROM in the box we can choose the **CDROM** option. We will then be prompted by a message that says **Please Insert the IPCop CDROM**

in the CDROM drive. This does not mean that the installation process didn't pick up the CD. Up until this point we could have been booting from a CD or a floppy and the installation process allows for this, if we hit **OK** installation should continue normally.

Hard Drive Partitioning and Formatting

We will then be warned that the system is about to partition and format the hard drive.

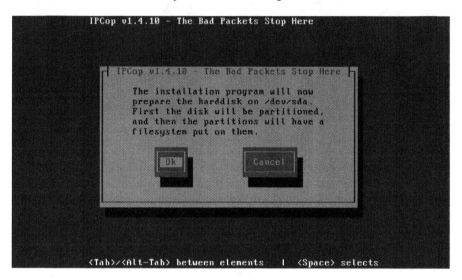

This is the point of no return and pressing *Enter* here wipes the disk entirely and we lose any data on the drive. As mentioned previously, as long as we have ensured that there is only one drive in the system and that the drive is the one we wouldn't mind wiping, we can continue. Pressing *Enter* will begin the partition and formatting process. This may take a minute or two if we have a large disk. It's generally a good idea to put a smaller disk in IPCop as it won't use a tremendous amount of space, depending upon how many log files we anticipate IPCop to have. We must ensure to meet the minimum requirements however, which is around 200 MB, while anything above 10 GB or so is highly unlikely to be used, unless you end up using add-ons that require more space—these add-ons will likely provide you with their disk space requirements.

Restore Configuration from Floppy Backup

At this stage we can choose to restore an earlier configuration saved on a floppy, which is an ideal way to back up an IPCop configuration.

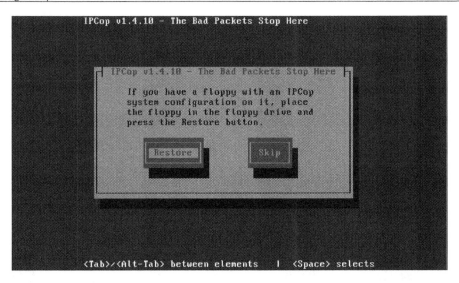

As this is our first IPCop installation, we are unlikely to have a floppy handy. However, if we did, we could choose to **Restore** and the rest of the system configuration would run automatically based on our previous installation options. For now we will choose to **Skip** this and carry on with a manual installation.

Green Interface Configuration

As we discussed in previous chapters, IPCop has a color scheme for referencing the NICs installed in the system. This is the first point in the installation process where we encounter these.

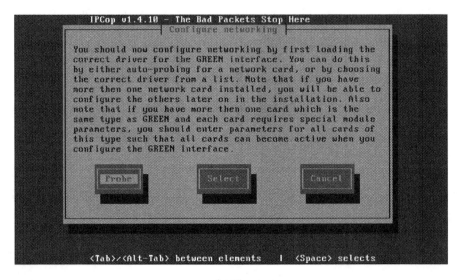

The Green interface corresponds to our local network and we can select this interface now. The simplest method is to allow IPCop to **Probe** for the network card, which it completes very reliably. If, however, we know exactly which make and model of card we want to use, we can choose to **Select** it manually which will then provide us with a list of known cards to choose from. This screen also makes reference to **special module parameters**, which are options we could pass to the network drivers in the kernel if necessary. Once this stage is configured, we can complete the rest of the installation remotely and we are asked to configure other cards later.

A slight complication at this stage is that the first card IPCop discovers will be used as the Green network interface if we let IPCop probe for the network cards. We may have a reason for picking a specific card for a specific interface: for instance, we might have a 10Mbit and a 100Mbit card, and wish to use the 10Mbit card for our internet connection. In this instance, we can employ one of two techniques—either to select the driver for the specific card we want as the Green interface ourselves, or to put the cards into the machine in order such that the Green card is in the lowest-numbered PCI or ISA slot. Also note that the name IPCop gives the card may not be the name of the make or model of the card as it relates to the **chipset** in use, for example many common cards will be identified as **Digital 21x4x Tulip PCI ....**.

Sometimes this can take a little work, and in particular, two identical network cards sharing the same box can cause confusion as to which network card is assigned to which interface. Some cards, such as older 3Com Etherlink cards, can be very hard to use when there is more than one of the card in the host. In a majority of these instances, assistance for the problem in particular can be found via the IPCop community.

Finished?

Wow that was easy! It seems we have finished the installation already.

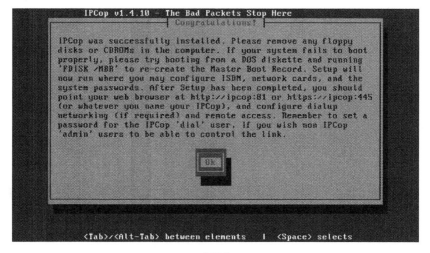

Don't get too carried away though; this message means that the base system files are in place and our most basic configuration has finished. We must now set up IPCop for our particular needs, by choosing which interface types we want to use and how our addressing system will work. Pressing *Enter* here will take us into the configuration of IPCop.

Locale Settings

We begin with our keyboard layout options.

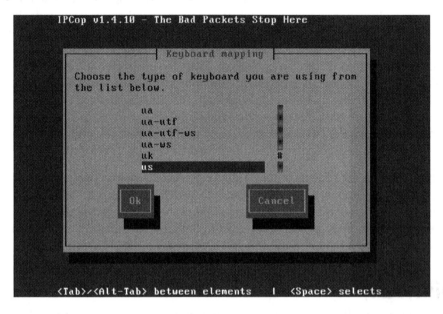

We should choose the keyboard layout we would like to use. For users with a standard US keyboard choose **us**, or **uk** for users with a UK layout. Choosing the wrong layout here could make menu navigation and commands a bit difficult later on, so be sure to choose the correct option. Check how your desktop system is configured if you are unsure.

We will also be prompted to choose our **Timezone** such as **GMT** or **EST**; again be careful to choose the correct option and check with your desktop system to see how it is configured.

Hostname

We now have to give the IPCop machine a name.

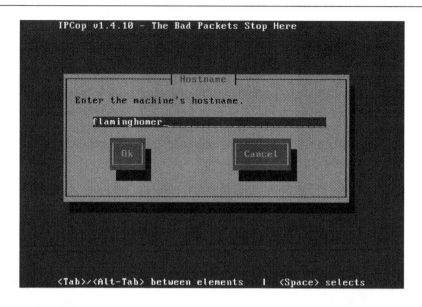

If we already have a naming scheme on the network we can use that; other options might be **firewall** or the default of **ipcop**. If we use the IPCop box as a DNS server it will reply with its own IP address for this name, so it can be convenient for addressing the web front-end of IPCop.

DNS Domain Name

The default domain name for IPCop on our local network is shown in the following figure:

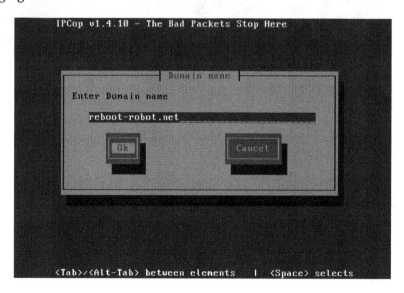

If we don't have one we can go with the default, although as a business network we may already have a domain we are using on our local segment; we should enter that here, being careful not to overlap internal and external DNS. For example if we are using **reboot-robot.net** externally, then using **lan.reboot-robot.net** internally may be be a better idea, to allow internal clients to reference both internal and external machines using DNS. Misconfiguring this, or using a domain name that does not belong to you, could result in that domain being inaccessible to clients inside the network. If we put **aol.com** in here, as an example, then we may have difficulty accessing AOL's website and other services.

ISDN Configuration

If we have an ISDN modem we can now configure it here:

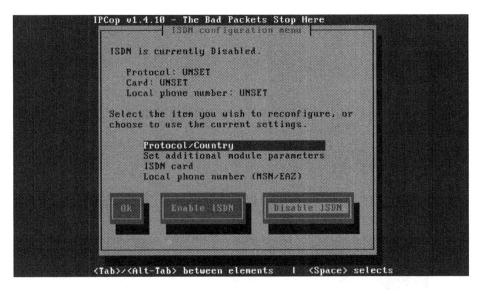

We will need the parameters such as the protocol in use and the phone number to use, all of this can be provided by the ISDN ISP. If you have to dial 9 for an outside line, then which should also be included and pauses can be added where necessary by inserting a comma. If we do not have ISDN we should choose to disable it; we can then set up other connection methods such as DSL in a later step.

Network Configuration

We should now be presented with the **Network configuration menu**.

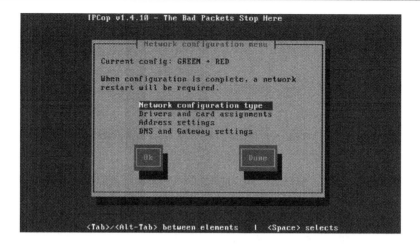

This is an important part of the setup process and directly relates to the network topologies we discussed in the previous chapter.

We first decide on our **Network configuration type**. There are many to choose from, and in the previous chapter we looked at an overview of a few of them. In this example, we will be running through the installation process for the **GREEN + RED** topology.

When we choose the appropriate option depending on the topology we decided upon in the previous chapter we can move on to the second item in the network configuration menu.

Drivers and Card Assignment

For each network interface card found in the system we will be prompted by a menu as shown in the following image:

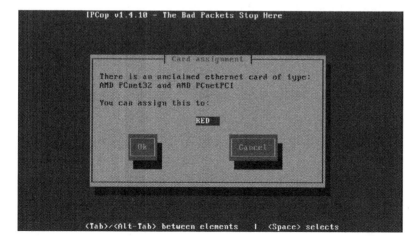

If we chose a topology with more interfaces, such as with Orange or Blue, we could assign the card to the interface we'd like it to be designated as. In the example shown above, we have one card and are assigning it to the **RED** interface; this will make it our Internet connection.

Address Settings

The next option in the network configuration menu is **Address Settings**. Here we can define which addresses we want to use on the server.

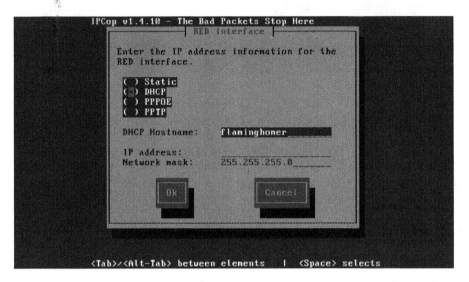

We always want the Green, Orange, and Blue interfaces to be static with a differing subnet for each interface. The Red interface will depend on our ISP, who will provide the configuration information. For Static, PPPOE, and PPTP, the addresses and configuration information should be configured as per your ISPs instructions. If we are using DHCP, however, all that is required is to click the **DHCP** option and leave all other settings at their defaults (unless instructed otherwise by your ISP). The majority of cable connections will use DHCP, while ADSL connections will vary depending upon what sort of ADSL router, modem, or interface card is used.

DNS and Default Gateway

We should also provide DNS and default gateway servers for use.

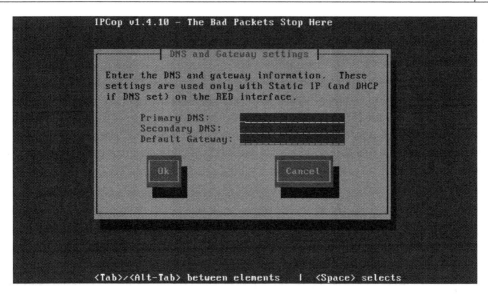

As noted, this is not always necessary for DHCP and is usually not a good idea as it will override the settings provided in DHCP by your ISP.

DHCP Server

If we decide to use IPCop for our DHCP, then we have to configure the various DHCP options.

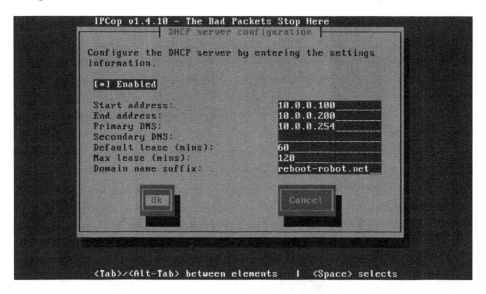

If we have a simple network with a couple of clients, we may want our IPCop to handle DHCP. In a larger network we may have a dedicated DHCP server in use already; if so we should disable the DHCP server.

DHCP requires a range of addresses to hand out to clients. We begin with providing this range, defined by a **Start address** and **End address**. In the case of the example above we have chosen **10.0.0.100** to **10.0.0.200**. **Default lease** and **Max lease** time is the duration we will allow DHCP clients to *lease* an IP address. There is generally no real reason to alter these unless your network has specific requirements for leases of a specified time.

Generally, as we've discussed earlier, we can pick any internal addressing scheme (as long as we use internal addresses) we want. As long as we are consistent in what we use, and configure everything sanely, this will all work, and the defaults from this example installation (apart from the domain name suffix, as we mentioned earlier) will work. Again, as we've discussed before, the only minor exception to this is if we have an ISP that uses these (RFC1918) addresses itself—this information can be obtained from your ISP.

Domain name suffix should be pre-populated with the information we provided earlier in the configuration and generally the suffix should go with other clients on the network to ensure that all clients are configured with identical settings, which also match the IPCop machine.

Finished!

Now we can get excited! We have finished the installation process of IPCop.

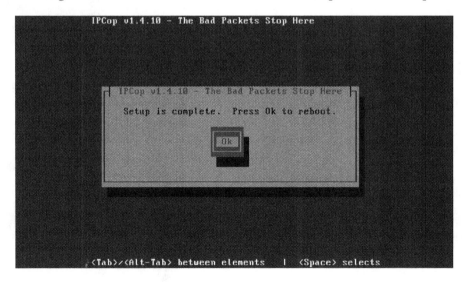

After pressing *Enter* here, the system will reboot into our IPCop installation for the first time.

First Boot

When the IPCop system boots up we will be shown the following screen, which is the boot loader installed as part of IPCop (Grub). We can now choose the boot option we want to use and optionally add any parameters to the kernel prior to boot. After a few seconds, the default entry should boot.

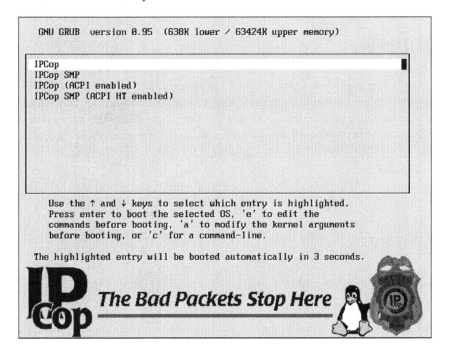

Grub

Grub is one of the commonly used boot loaders for Linux, and it essentially intermediates between the computer's BIOS and the operating system, letting us choose multiple operating systems or just specify options for one (such as picking SMP or ACPI support rather than the standard kernel, as in the menu shown in the previous screenshot).

More information on Grub can be found on the FSF website.

http://www.gnu.org/software/grub/

We should then see some boot information output on the screen, which should last for a few seconds, followed by a satisfying set of happy beeps and finally the following output:

```
IPCop v1.4.10 - The Bad Packets Stop Here
flaminghomer login:
```

This is the Linux login prompt and signifies that we have now installed and successfully booted the IPCop system. IPCop will now function as a basic NAT firewall for us, without the need for further configuration.

Summary

In this chapter we covered getting an IPCop system up and running with the configurations and topologies we covered previously. We also saw that NAT should be passing through the firewall; clients should be able to obtain IP addresses, use DNS, and access the Internet. We can now go on to customize the system and enable features and services that aren't available by default. In the next few chapters we will cover basic configuration and then look at more advanced options such as Intrusion Detection and VPNs.

5
Basic IPCop Usage

Now that we have covered the installation of the IPCop firewall and several situations in which we would want to deploy it, we can discuss how to administer and operate an IPCop firewall. Assuming that the installation has been successful, a default IPCop installation presents us with a web interface. The web interface allows us to configure the firewall via any web browser, and is (by default) enabled only for clients on the Green, internal interface.

The web server runs on port 445 (for **HTTPS** traffic) by default, although these ports can be altered; the port is different from the commonly used/allocated port (443). It should be noted that accessing the web interface using this port will yield a certificate popup—this results from the use of a self-signed **SSL** certificate, and can safely be ignored.

The port assignment for HTTPS administration can be changed to any port above 445 using the `setreservedports` command from the IPCop console or an **SSH** session, and this may be a consideration for anyone who wishes to access their IPCop host remotely, as some Internet Service Providers will firewall traffic to port 445 in order to prevent worms such as Sasser, which exploit vulnerabilities in Windows over port 445 (**SMB** over **TCP**). Alteration of this port to below 445 must be done manually, although it should not be undertaken lightly, and will require the editing of the same files as `setreservedports` (`http://www.ipcop.org/modules.php?op=modload&name=phpWiki&file=index&pagename=IPCop140HttpsPortHowto`).

Unencrypted traffic to port 81, supported in versions pre-1.4, is deprecated, and existed initially only to support browsers without support for HTTPS/SSL. Since version 1.4 of the IPCop firewall, this has been altered in order to allow only HTTPS administration (although port 81 can be reconfigured).

Accessing our IPCop firewall via `https://ipcopfirewall:445/` (where ipcopfirewall is the name or IP address of the host), then, gives us the default configuration screen with an overview of the status of the IPCop firewall, the update status, system load, and menus for all of the appropriate configuration options. Any messages about certificates at this point can be safely ignored, and stem from the fact that your IPCop host generates its own SSL certificate, rather than using one issued by a **Certificate Authority (CA)** your browser may know about, such as VeriSign or CAcert.

The System Menu

The items in the **System** menu are fairly critical to the system's functionality.

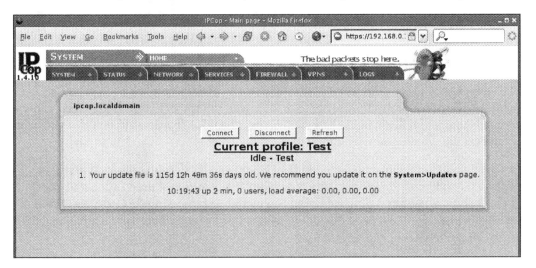

Software Updates

The first thing we should do, post-installation, is to ensure that our IPCop firewall has the appropriate updates applied. Although many software updates provide updates and bug fixes for new features and existing software packages, some address new security issues, and in order to maintain the integrity of the firewall; it is important to apply these as frequently as possible.

The Software Updates functionality is provided under the **System | Updates** menu.

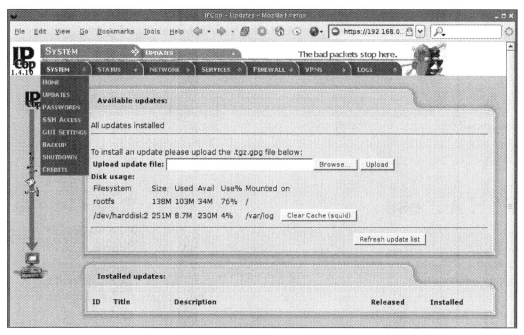

The **Refresh update list** button connects to the IPCop servers and retrieves a list of released updates—the **Available updates** portion of the page will indicate when there are updates that need to be supplied, and provide a download link. The updates must be manually downloaded as-is (not unpacked or extracted) from the Internet and then uploaded (via the **Browse** button) to the firewall.

As the name of the update files (`*.tgz.gpg`) indicates, the updates are signed with, the **GNU Privacy Guard** (**GPG**), which prevents unauthorized (or compromised) updates from being issued by anyone without first compromising the IPCop key used to sign the updates. The GPG signature prevents unpacking and reassembly or modification of the updates, causing IPCop to refuse to use an update file that has either been tampered with by an intruder or unpacked instead of being simply downloaded and uploaded.

The update will indicate whether a restart of the IPCop firewall is required, but in many instances, it is not, and it is typically kernel updates that require this.

Some releases of the IPCop firewall (generally major version increments, such as 1.3-1.4) require that the firewall be completely reinstalled, as the upgrade procedure is too complex to be carried out via an update as with a minor version increment. In this case, the firewall configuration can be backed up, so the firewall is not being entirely rebuilt from scratch.

Passwords

The next **System** menu allows us to alter passwords—this screen is relatively self-explanatory, giving us the option to reset the **admin** password (which gives complete control over the web interface) and the **dial** password. The **dial** user allows a user access only to connect or disconnect a connection, which must be manually dialed, such as an analog modem.

The third account on the system, the root account (whose password you set during the installation), has the power to reset both the **admin** and **dial** user account passwords, but this facility must be used either on the console of the IPCop firewall or via SSH, which must be manually enabled.

SSH Access

SSH access allows us to securely establish a console session using an account with the appropriate privileges (such as the root account) remotely. SSH is a very useful tool, and a thorough coverage of it is beyond the scope of this chapter or even this book. At its most basic, SSH may be used to run commands and administer the system in a manner (i.e. textually, at the command line) similar to that done on the console of the machine itself.

Within the context of IPCop this is extremely useful because we can run the setup program, which we ran during the installation procedure (allowing us to reset or alter parameters such as the network configuration and card allocation, or reset passwords). If you altered the topology of your network or added/replaced network cards in your IPCop firewall, you might want to reconfigure it via SSH.

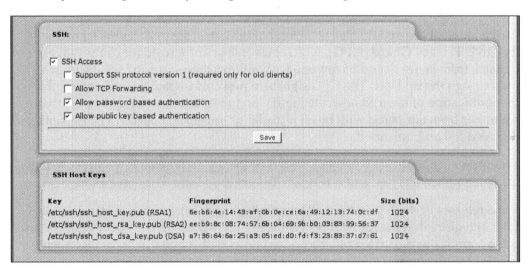

SSH Keys

http://hacks.oreilly.com/pub/h/66 is a good brief overview of the use of SSH keys, along with a few pointers to other resources (and a wide collection of user comments on the topic).

Key authentication allows the use of keys stored on client computers (in a similar manner to SSL) to authenticate clients, rather than passwords that are transmitted (over an encrypted tunnel) over the Internet each time they are used during the SSH authentication phase (SSH-USERAUTH). This authentication method, assuming that the key is not stolen or compromised, is significantly more secure than the use of passwords, but more complex to understand and configure, and a little less flexible (a key file is required on any system you want to use to log in to your SSH server, whereas a password only needs to be remembered).

SSH is also more useful generally as a diagnostic tool—there are many tools included with IPCop that can only be accessed via the command line, such as `vim` (a powerful text editor), network utilities such as `ping` and `traceroute`, and `tcpdump`, which is extremely useful for debugging networking issues by dumping network traffic or just viewing the headers on the console. We can also use many of the standard Unix utilities such as `touch` and `grep`. Many of these (in fact all the commands mentioned in this paragraph apart from `vim` and `tcpdump`) are provided by `busybox`, the program that runs to provide the shell used when you log in at the console or via SSH.

The Busybox Shell

Learn more about the `busybox` shell and the options it provides at: http://www.busybox.net/downloads/BusyBox.html.

Connecting to SSH

Accessing SSH on a Linux or Unix system is fairly easy—once we have enabled SSH, it runs on the (non-default) port 222, so a command similar to the following will get you into your IPCop host (assuming a hostname of "IPCop"):

```
james@horus: - $ ssh -p 222 root@ipcop
root@ipcop's password:
Last login: Thu Feb 27 12:31:22 2006 from 10.0.2.241
root@ipcop:- #
```

At this point, you can work as if you were logged into the machine. On the Windows platform, an excellent free SSH client exists called **PuTTY**, whilst Linux and recent Unix platforms such as OS X almost universally have a command-line SSH client installed. In OS X this is accessible via `Terminal.app`, while konsole, gnome-terminal, rxvt, or any other Linux terminal emulator may be used in any recent Linux desktop to use SSH.

Download PuTTY

Download PuTTY from
`http://www.chiark.greenend.org.uk/~sgtatham/`
`putty/download.html`

To use PuTTY, launch the `putty.exe` file downloaded from the above URL. This should pop up a box similar to the one shown in the following figure:

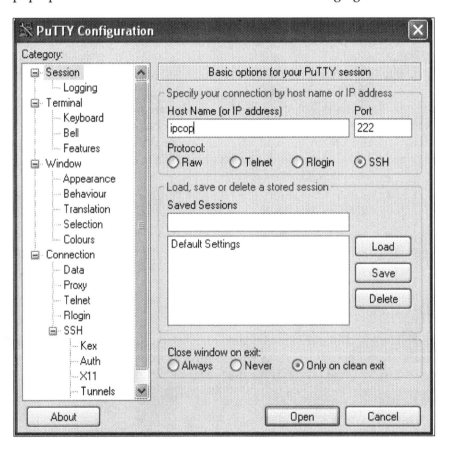

To connect to an IPCop host, enter the hostname or IP address of the host into the **Host Name** box, and the port number **222** into the **Port** box. You can save these settings by entering a profile name into the **Saved Sessions** textbox and clicking **Save**; the next time you open PuTTY, there will be an entry listed in the multi-list box, which presently only says **Default Settings**, with the name you entered into the **Saved Sessions** box. You can simply double-click this entry to connect. Use the username **root** and the password you set during the installation to connect, and you should have a prompt very similar to the one listed previously on a Linux system.

A Little More about SSH

SSH itself is a mature protocol in very wide deployment, and as such poses a minimal (and well understood) security risk. It is designed and maintained by the OpenSSH team, well known for OpenBSD, which has a reputation as one of the most secure operating systems in the world. As such, if you do not have a requirement for the form of richer VPN connectivity that the VPN functionality in IPCop can provide, SSH offers a lower profile alternative (and peace of mind).

SSH also provides us with several other powerful tools—the SSH protocol includes functionality that allows network connections to be tunneled over SSH (**TCP forwarding**). By enabling this option on our IPCop firewall and exposing SSH to the outside world, we have a very lightweight, platform-independent way to access internal network resources, and/or the IPCop configuration page without the overhead or complexity of a VPN.

This might, for instance, be a great way to access a customer's machine internally while it sits behind an IPCop firewall, or to simply access the IPCop web interface without exposing the web server to the Internet.

Using SSH to Tunnel Network Traffic

Briefly, there are several ways to use SSH via our IPCop firewall in order to tunnel network traffic. With TCP forwarding enabled, we can use **Dynamic port forwarding** to send connections through the SSH session via a proxy server. Using the command-line version of SSH, we do this using a command similar to the following:

```
james@horus: ~ $ ssh -D 1234 -p 222
root@80.68.90.223

root@ipcop's password:

Last login: Thu Mar 2 10:22:42 2006 from
207.46.250.119

root@ipcop:~ #
```

As long as we leave this SSH connection open (and we can use it as an ordinary SSH connection), our local machine (i.e. the system we initiated the connection on) will have a proxy server running on the loopback interface (i.e. listening only on the address 127.0.0.1) and on port 1234. We can then use any proxy-aware application to connect to any host that the IPCop host can connect to. This can be a poor man's VPN, used to access websites privately on a public internet connection, or as mentioned above, we can use it to access the web interface on the IPCop host or internal network resources.

The SSH man page is extremely comprehensive—man ssh on any Linux/Unix system (apart from IPCop) or a Google search for "man ssh" will provide a comprehensive listing of the other options available with the ssh command. PuTTY also supports similar options (including dynamic port forwarding in the same manner) via the GUI.

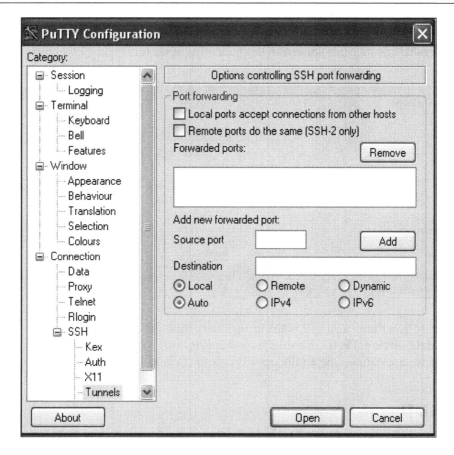

Enter the port you wish to use on the client for proxying connections into the **Source port** box, pick **Dynamic**, hit **Add**, and then connect as normal. Once this has been configured for a specific connection, this setting will be saved along with the hostname and port number if you choose to save your profile in PuTTY.

SSH and TCP Forwarding

http://www.securityfocus.com/infocus/1816 is an excellent security focus article written by Brian Hatch in 2005 about SSH's capabilities in this area. It is complex, but well worth reading if you are even remotely interested in this topic.

The **SSH Access** page also lets us view the SSH keys. Use of these is strongly encouraged — but beyond the scope of this book. Again, the SSH documentation (and the SSH man pages) is strongly encouraged as a good source of information on this.

GUI Settings

The **GUI Settings** menu is shown in the following image:

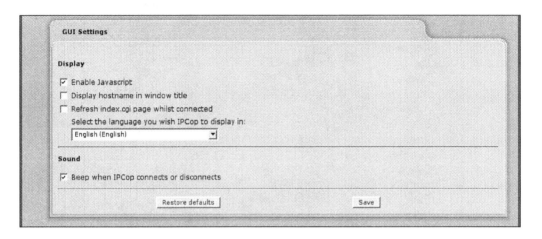

The only option that we might want to seriously look at (and which isn't immediately obvious) is the **Enable Javascript** option, which we might want to disable if we are connecting to IPCop with older (or text-mode) clients.

Backup

We can use the **Backup menu** in IPCop to back up our settings to a floppy disk or to a file accessible via the network. Apart from being useful for disaster recovery purposes, this also forms an important part of the upgrade procedure between major version increments where an in-place upgrade is not always possible (and the firewall must be reinstalled and the configuration restored).

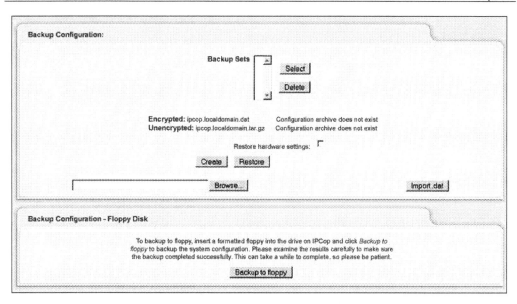

The **Backup Configuration:** option at the top allows us to create backups on the IPCop host itself—hitting the **Create** button allows us to create a backup that is listed under **Backup Sets**.

Backup Encryption

As of version IPCop 1.4.0, backup functionality with encryption written by Tim Butterfield is included in IPCop. When IPCop makes encrypted backups, it does so using a random key stored on the machine itself, required to restore the backup. If your backups are encrypted, you will require a copy of the key to restore the backup.

For more information on how this works, see the author's original page on the backup add-on prior to integration into the main body of IPCop code:

http://www.timbutterfield.com/computer/
ipcop/backup.php

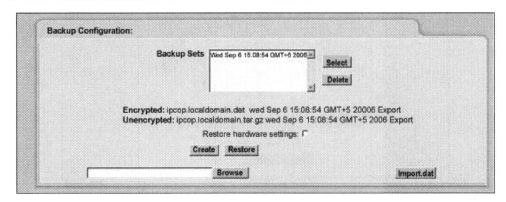

By picking the backup in question and clicking on **Select**, we can download the appropriate backups and save them for archiving on another machine, or to a CD, tape, etc. As there is limited space on many IPCop firewalls, this allows the maintenance of a comprehensive backup set in a manner that does not compromise operational efficiency (and in a manner which is more disaster-tolerant than simply storing the backups on the same host). As firewall configuration tends to remain relatively static, a backup regimen for an IPCop host may not need to be frequent, but for obvious reasons, a regular backup schedule (or a procedure for backing up after each significant change) is strongly recommended.

Shutdown

The **Shutdown:** menu is relatively straightforward, allowing a manual restart or shutdown of the IPCop host, and also allowing us to schedule a periodic restart of the host.

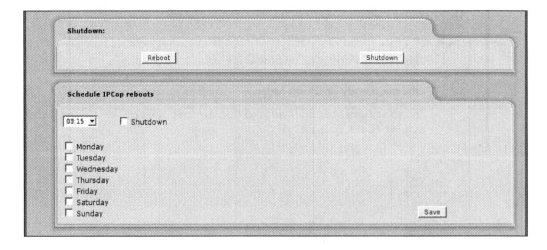

Checking the Status of Our IPCop Firewall

Part of our management procedures should include monitoring of the IPCop firewall in order to ensure that CPU load, memory usage, network throughput, etc., maintain healthy levels. It is an extremely important role of the system administrator to establish a **baseline** for his or her systems in order to be able to identify abnormalities—many intrusions and hardware failures are first noticed by a drop (or rise) in network activity or CPU load.

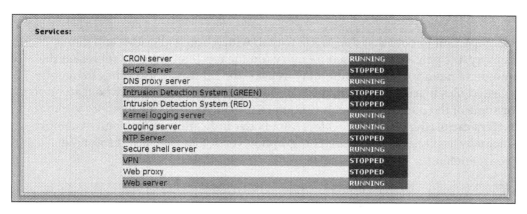

The basic status screen allows us to view a number of basic system statistics before we inspect more detailed graphs of the statistics for the lifetime of the firewall. Services running on the IPCop box obviously have a serious impact on the ability of the box to do its job, and as a quick indicator the **Services:** display is useful in the event that the firewall ceases to function properly in order to ensure that the firewall thinks that the right services are running.

Many of the services, such as **Secure shell server** and the **Web proxy**, are not running by default—the previous image illustrates the default settings with the addition of the SSH server (which we enabled earlier in the chapter).

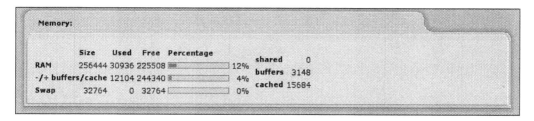

Memory: is fairly self-evident. Performance issues, particularly in a host that is a web proxy for larger networks — may be caused by inadequate memory. Although not always an indicator of memory issues, particularly if a host is under heavy load and in use by some of the more intensive functionality IPCop provides (such as the proxy server), the **Swap** indicator is worth understanding. **Swapping** is the process by which memory allocated to processes is moved to the hard drive, rather than being stored in the system's **Random Access Memory**. This effectively allows the system to operate with more physical memory than the host has, at the cost of speed when the swapping operation is performed; accessing data on the hard disk for a program whose memory has been *swapped out* is significantly slower than accessing it from *real* memory.

It is important to note that due to the way in which Linux allocates and manages memory, the percentage of used memory (on the top line) does *not* represent the amount of memory that is immutably in use — the Linux kernel caches frequently accessed files in a **disk cache** in memory to improve performance, which accounts for some of the memory usage. It is often more sane to view the memory without **buffers/cache** (the second indicator) for a better indication of how much memory is actually *available*. This is a prettier, graphed version of the output from the `free` command.

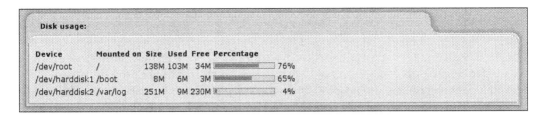

Disk usage: for your IPCop system should also be relatively self-evident. The **/boot** partition is used to store the Operating System kernel and configuration information (since this is managed as part of the software update process, the usage isn't critical even at high levels). The largest partition, used for the only thing that really grows, is mounted to **/var/log**, and as the name indicates, is used for storing log files.

```
Uptime and users:

 10:28:48 up 11 min,  0 users,  load average: 0.00, 0.00, 0.00
 USER     TTY      LOGIN@   IDLE   JCPU   PCPU WHAT
```

Uptime and users: Uptime is self-evident. Users might not be; since this is (literally) the output from the w command, **users** refers to users logged into the Linux host itself, via an interactive session on the console or SSH. This should not be taken to mean that no one is *using* IPCop as a firewall, proxy server, or logged in via the web interface.

Load in this context is, in accordance with the w command, *Unix* load. The three numbers that are listed represent load for the last 1, 5, and 15 minutes respectively. The number represents the number of processes using or waiting for CPU time, or in an uninterruptible sleep. Each such process adds 1 to the load number, and the number you see is an average of this for the period in question.

Load is not always a good measure of the load of the box, and network throughput, specific CPU statistics, and a more fine-grained output detailing process-specific information is often far more useful as a diagnostic tool (rather than a rough indicator).

```
Loaded modules:

Module           Size  Used by     Not tainted
ipt_mark          440   1 (autoclean)
ipt_TCPMSS       2200   1 (autoclean)
ipt_state         504  15 (autoclean)
ipt_REJECT       3000   1 (autoclean)
ipt_LOG          3776   9 (autoclean)
ipt_limit         888  10 (autoclean)
iptable_mangle   2008   1 (autoclean)
iptable_filter   1612   1 (autoclean)
```

Loaded modules: is another piece of operating system–specific information. The Linux kernel bundles pieces of functionality as loadable *modules*, which may be removed or just not loaded if they aren't necessary. Each piece of functionality that is modular and in use will show up here; the majority of these will be loaded at startup time, and represent everything from device drivers for network cards to the modules required by iptables to perform different firewalling functions (some of which are displayed in the previous figure).

Unless you have a specific need to understand or view which modules are in use (or are just curious), this is not terribly useful information. The previous figure is essentially the output of the lsmod command.

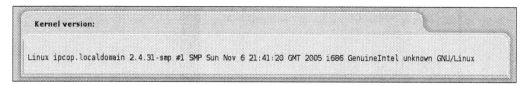

```
Kernel version:

Linux ipcop.localdomain 2.4.31-smp #1 SMP Sun Nov 6 21:41:20 GMT 2005 i686 GenuineIntel unknown GNU/Linux
```

This is the output of the command `uname -a`, which displays, from left to right: Kernel name, Network node hostname, Kernel release, Kernel version, Machine hardware name, and Operating System.

Network Status

The information contained on the **Network Status** screen is frequently very useful in troubleshooting networking issues.

The first tool we are given is a colorized version of the output from the `ifconfig` command, with the network interfaces on the system being given the colors that IPCop uses to refer to them. Quite often when the IPCop host is attached to a network such as a Cable or ADSL connection that allocates configuration information via DHCP, this can be useful for verifying whether a loss of connectivity is related to the IPCop host or if there is a network outage with the service provider. Since we can see the number of errors and dropped packets, this can frequently be useful in troubleshooting other networking issues too.

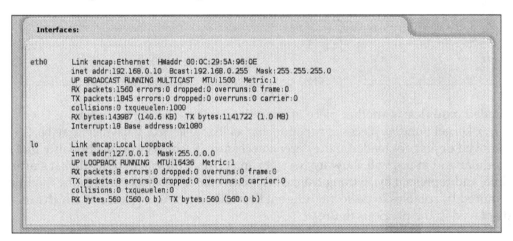

The **lo** interface represents the **Local Loopback** adapter, with the address of **127.0.0.1**, and should always be present. On this system, the Red interface is inactive, but on a fully populated IPCop system, we could see up to five interfaces here (Red, Green, Orange, Blue, and loopback).

IP Address	MAC Address	Hostname	Lease expires (local time d/m/y)
192.168.0.159	00:0c:29:15:d6:7f	Knoppix	02/03/2006 12:44:59
192.168.0.160	00:50:56:c0:00:01		02/03/2006 11:44:00

Current dynamic leases

The **Current dynamic leases** table is actually showing us the *DHCP* leases handed out to clients on the internal network segments. In this case we have two clients, one of them has not provided a hostname with the DHCP request, and the other (**Knoppix**) has. IPCop registers hostnames with DNS, so the host **Knoppix** should be addressable as **Knoppix** via IPCop's DNS server.

Expired leases are scored through (struck out). The output displayed here essentially consists of the contents of /var/state/dhcp/dhcpd.leases.

Apart from letting us debug DHCP, this is also a quick and useful way to get hold of the MAC address for specific systems, either for setting up static reservations or for any other purpose.

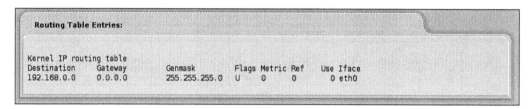

The routing table is used by the firewall to determine where to forward (or send) IP datagrams being handled by the system. A full discussion of routing is beyond the scope of this book, but the host routing table is an excellent first port of call for many networking issues, and a thorough understanding of routing is vital for the efficient administration of a firewall, network, or even a set of workstations.

The ARP table consists of the current mappings between IP addresses and hardware (MAC) addresses on the local network segment(s). There are generally entries for each client on the network as well as one for the upstream router (either a Cable/ADSL router, or more usually the ISP's upstream router). As with many other items, this is extremely useful for some aspects of network troubleshooting, but beyond the scope of this book.

System Graphs

IPCop uses a package called **rrdtool** (http://oss.oetiker.ch/rrdtool/) to maintain a set of graphs of a number of statistics pertaining to the system and network activity. These are automatically set up when the system is installed, and statistics we have access to under the **System Graphs** menu are **CPU Usage**, **Memory Usage**, **Swap Usage**, and **Disk Access**.

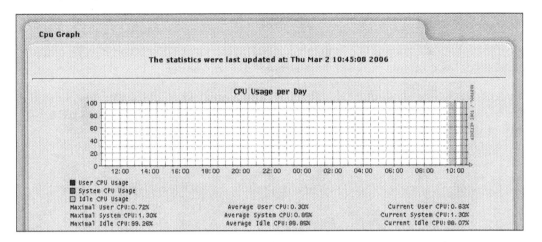

The previous figure is an example of such a graph (for CPU usage). Clicking on a specific graph drills down on that particular statistic, giving you graphs detailing that metric for the last day, week, month, and year.

You should note that due to **UTF** issues with rrdtool (which prevents the use of special characters), IPCop is currently constrained to generating these graphs in English only.

Network Graphs

IPCop also maintains graphs of network traffic across the interfaces in the system. These work in an identical manner to **System Graphs**.

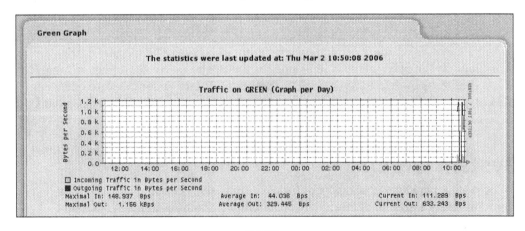

Connections

The **Connections** feature displays a colorized output detailing all of the connections presently made through the IPCop firewall. Clicking on an IP Address in this screen performs a **reverse DNS lookup** on the address, giving you the hostname associated with the address if reverse DNS is configured (i.e. if the address has a **PTR** record).

Services

Although IPCop is a firewall package, it contains many pieces of functionality that are outside the scope of a plain firewall. DNS and DHCP functionality, for instance, are normally served by separate hosts. IPCop, designed for smaller deployments in which half a dozen different servers (router, firewall, DHCP server, DNS server, Proxy server, IDS, etc.) are simply not feasible, bundles all of this functionality together.

The **Services** tab is where we can configure many of the features in IPCop that are separate elements, and require more complex setup. Some of these are covered in their own chapter; others, which are almost always deployed with IPCop (such as DNS and DHCP), will be covered here.

DHCP Server

The top of the **DHCP Server** page allows us to reconfigure some of the options we set up when we installed IPCop (such as the start and end address and lease time). Others, such as options for **WINS** servers and the option for **Additional DHCP Options**, can now be added to our configuration.

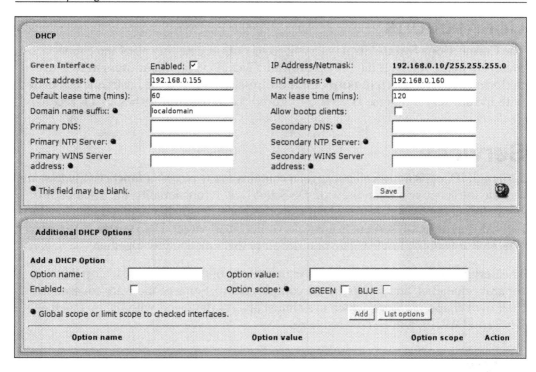

If you do not understand DHCP, you probably have no need to reconfigure this (if your IPCop box is functioning as expected). You would, however, be well advised to understand DHCP (and the various flaws that it has).

Further down the page, we can configure **fixed leases**. Fixed leases (sometimes referred to as reservations) allow you to configure the DHCP server to respond with a specific IP address (rather than a random address from the pool) for a host matching a certain MAC address. The benefit of this is that you can have the power that centrally managing your IP configuration gives you while having the ability to reliably make connections to hosts by IP address rather than relying on DNS.

For some devices, such as network printers or IP cameras, that frequently do not handle dynamic DNS (or use an unfriendly and often unchangeable hostname), this is godsend if you don't want to manually set IP addresses statically on every networked device on your network.

Below this, we can (again) see the **Current dynamic leases**. This is a useful inclusion, if we have just attached a DHCP-capable device to our network but want to allocate it a specific address; we can copy the MAC address, create a fixed lease for it, and restart the device—at which point it should reacquire the correct (static) address.

The **Root Path** and **Filename** options, which may be unfamiliar to many network administrators or IT Professionals, are used for configuring systems booting from the network and reading files via **NFS**. In the vast majority of deployments (as the page indicates), it is safe to ignore them

Dynamic DNS

Many internet connections in smaller businesses or at home use dynamically assigned IP addresses, via protocols such as PPP or DHCP, from a pool owned by the ISP. This enables the ISP to minimize the number of IP addresses it requires (as theoretically, it only needs as many IP addresses as the maximum number of clients online at any given time) and makes centralized configuration easier.

As a client's IP address will typically change session-for-session, as is the case with dial-up, or at indeterminate intervals, as is the case with ADSL or Cable clients, incoming connections are a problem. There is no way to get a client to VPN into the IPCop server, or deliver mail to the site the IPCop host exists on, if the IP address is constantly changing.

Dynamic DNS Providers solve this problem. By using an agent on the client machine that constantly updates a server on the Internet, the Dynamic DNS Provider can update a DNS name (such as youripcopserver.afraid.org) with the current IP address, so that as long as the IPCop host remains online, clients can always connect to it via the same DNS name.

IPCop has support for an extensive list of Dynamic DNS Providers, most of which are free. Afraid.org (`http://freedns.afraid.org/`) is an excellent choice, and has a reliable and well-setup service. All of the dynamic DNS providers work in fundamentally the same way—you register an account via the provider's website, and then provide IPCop with the details such that it can register itself. At this point (and given a minute or two for everything to start working) the hostname you registered for should resolve to your IPCop's Red IP address. Generally speaking, this is very simple and straightforward.

If you want to test this externally but do not have an external host to do it from, there are several online DNS testing services such as `www.dnsstuff.com` that you can use in order to look up the **A** record for your domain in order to see if it resolves to the right IP address.

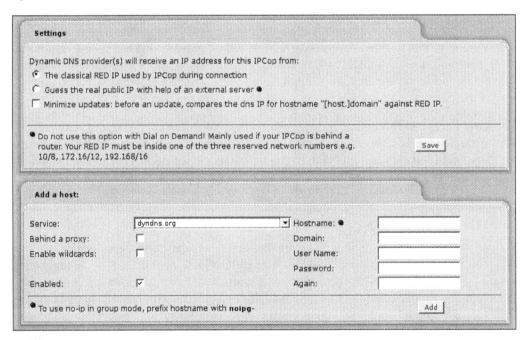

Generally speaking, the **The classical RED IP used by IPCop during connection** option, which is checked by default will be the most appropriate option for you. If your IPCop router is behind another router, you will experience problems in actually connecting to the IPCop box via the Internet, and even more problems in connecting to internal services, as your traffic will effectively be undergoing Network Address Translation twice. The recommended solution if (as the page suggests) you are behind another NAT router is to remove that other NAT router and plug the IPCop Red interface directly into your internet connection if you're able to do so.

Configuring Port Forwarding

Note that in order to be able to connect to your IPCop host (or any resources behind it) you will have to configure port forwards to internal services in addition to being able to resolve the IP address of your IPCop host from the Internet.

Some routers for which this is not possible (such as Ethernet ADSL modems) will allow you to enable a bridged mode instead of performing NAT themselves. ADSL Routers using Conexant chipsets (among others) have a half-bridge feature that passes along the IP address received from the ADSL provider to the first computer plugged into the router's Ethernet port(s) via DHCP. This is a hack, but a useful one, as it allows one host to be directly connected to the Internet without the need for complex setups.

You should consult your manufacturer's documentation or support service for information on setting this up, as this is a fairly complex topic that varies greatly from router to router.

Dynamic DNS

Note that the phrase **Dynamic DNS** refers to two things within the context of this book. One, mentioned here, refers to the IP address of the IPCop host being registered with a provider on the Internet in order that the clients on the Internet can find the IPCop host via a predictable hostname (such as *youripcopbox.afraid.org*) even when the IP address changes.

The second, mentioned elsewhere, refers to the process by which clients in the IPCop Green network register *their* hostnames with the IPCop DNS Service in order that other machines on the IPCop internal segments can resolve their IP addresses from their hostnames. This second service is strictly internal and has no direct bearing on the outside world.

Edit Hosts

The hosts file, present in Linux/Unix as /etc/hosts and in Windows as %SystemRoot%\System32\Drivers\Hosts, provides a means to manually set hostname-IP address relationships without the need for DNS. This can be useful for testing purposes, as a backup to DNS, or in environments with no DNS. In the event that you needed to force IPCop to resolve a particular hostname to a specific IP address, you could do so here without the need for a complex DNS configuration. This is something that you should not play with unless you have a good understanding of what it does.

Time Server

NTP is a protocol designed to synchronize time from the Internet. Very simply, your IPCop host connects to a Stratum 2 NTP server and ascertains the time; this Stratum 2 NTP server itself connects to a Stratum 1 server (or more than one) in order to maintain its time source to an acceptable level of accuracy.

The Stratum 1 server(s) maintain their time against an external time source such as a GPS clock, or radio receiver. This divide is maintained in order to reduce the load on the Stratum 1 servers, which would otherwise be unable to cope with the number of clients. It is considered as a bad practice to synchronize your server to a Stratum 1 NTP source unless you have a large (numbered in the thousands) network. You should also try to pick a Stratum 2 server (or pool) that is as close to you as possible, because the closer the server is, the more accurately your system will be able to set its clock.

Accurate time is extremely important for networked devices and in particular for firewalls, as being able to accurately discern the order in which logged events (such as intrusions) occurred is often crucial for maintaining a functional infrastructure and investigating (and prosecuting) intruders.

NTP generally maintains an accuracy level of between 5-15 milliseconds over the Internet. A detailed explanation of where NTP originated, why it is important, along with a list of available NTP servers, is available online at http://ntp.isc.org/bin/view/Main/WebHome.

IPCop has the ability to synchronize to an external NTP source and also provide an NTP service for the clients on the local network.

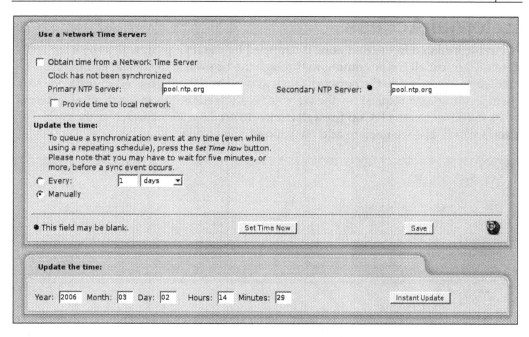

The default settings, if you check the **Obtain time from a Network Time Server** setting, should work—but you are recommended to pick a **Primary NTP Server** (or pool) that is closer to you. As the configuration page indicates, IPCop can also automatically synchronize the time.

IPCop will also let you set the time via the web interface. This is useful for an initial installation if the system clock is particularly out of sync, as an NTP update may not occur straightaway if you synchronize manually. If you do not wish to use NTP for whatever reason, you can keep your time updated in this way—or just use it to test NTP by setting the time incorrectly and then verifying whether NTP does indeed work.

Firewall Functionality

The **Firewall** drop-down menu in IPCop contains functionality to configure functions of the firewall itself. Since IPCop's design philosophy is to treat the Green zone as implicitly trusted and downgrade trust from there onwards, there is no egress filtering natively built into IPCop. Instead, your two main choices for configuration here are **External Access**, which lets you control which ports IPCop will allow in the inbound direction, and **Port Forwarding**. See Chapter 9 for more information on setting up a more granular firewall policy, particularly for egress traffic (i.e. traffic traversing from Green to Red).

External Access

All traffic initiated in the Red zone is dropped by the IPCop firewall's rules by default. Almost all traffic coming in through the firewall in response to a request made by a client inside the network (such as a website being served in response to a client sending a *get* request for the website) is allowed, but in order to allow external hosts to connect to the IPCop firewall itself—to access a service such as the web interface or SSH—we need to add an external access rule.

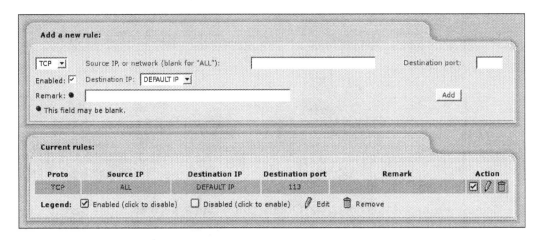

As we can see, IPCop by default has only one external access rule, for port 113 (ident). Although there is no service running on this port by default on the IPCop Host, this rule exists in order to allow services that make connections to ident (such as IRC or Internet Relay Chat) to connect without waiting for the connection to timeout. By opening this port via external access, any connection to ident on the IPCop firewall will meet with a closed port, speeding up the connection compared to a filtered port.

By default, then, if we add an allow rule, traffic destined for the allowed port will hit that port on IPCop's external interface. The **External Access** screen lets us allow traffic in through IPCop's outermost defenses—actually port forwarding (or allowing the traffic to hit a specific internal machine) is done in the next section.

Port Forwarding

Since we only have one external (Red) IP address and multiple internal clients, in order to allow a connection to a specific port on a specific internal machine from the Internet, we have to assign a port on the Red interface to correspond with the service on the internal machine, and *forward* this traffic to the client internally.

Under certain circumstances, such as if we were publishing an internal SSH (22) server to the web, we might choose to use a different external port to the port listening on the internal host. We might, for instance, port forward port 4022 on the firewall to port 22 on the internal host. The benefits of this approach are that we can accommodate many instances of the same service (using ports 4023, 4024, etc.) and that there is a slight security benefit in hiding the port our SSH service is running on.

One major disadvantage of this approach is that in some circumstances, the port is critical for the application running on it. HTTP traffic, for instance, defaults to port 80 — the browser requires an extra parameter (usually denoted by a colon followed by the port number at the end of the IP address or hostname) to access HTTP traffic on an alternative port, as is the case with IPCop's own relocated HTTP/HTTPS interfaces on port 81 and 445.

If we relocate HTTP traffic to port 81 (or another port), clients behind a firewall allowing connections only to port 80 may also be inadvertently prevented from accessing our web server.

Some services require a specific port number. If we have an internal mail server to which we forward port 25 (SMTP) from our IPCop firewall, we must use port 25 externally or mail servers relaying mail to us will not be able to connect to the mail server — SMTP servers use port 25, and no means exist for using an alternative port on the Web.

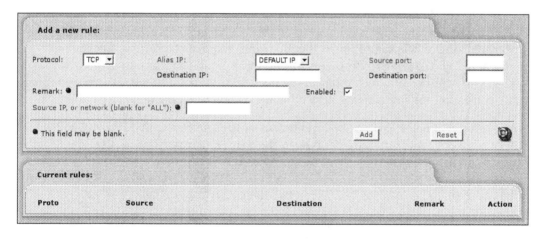

Our **Source port**, then, refers to the port that we open on the external interface. The **Destination port** refers to the port on the target host. If we wanted to forward port 4022 externally to port 22 on the internal host 10.1.1.123, for instance, we would enter **4022** into the **Source port** box, **22** into the **Destination port** box, and **10.1.1.123** into the **Destination IP** box.

Forwarding Multiple Ports

You can forward multiple consecutive ports by specifying a port range. This is accomplished through use of colons to delineate between the lowest and highest port in the range. If, for instance, we wanted to port forward ports 10 to 30 on the external interface to ports 10 to 30 on a server within the network, we would put **10:30** in **Source port** and **10:30** in **Destination port**.

The **Source IP, or network (blank for "ALL")** box allows us to accept connections only from specific hosts. We might want to do this if we were opening up a protocol such as **RDP (3389)** to the Web, which we were not entirely happy with the security of. Alternatively, we may choose to actively allow connections only from trusted IP blocks as a matter of course, and pursue this approach for all of our port forwarding rules (apart from SMTP , which requires that connections be made to it by so many different hosts that setting up IP-based filtering in this manner is virtually impossible).

We might want to choose a different *protocol* if we were port forwarding a protocol such as DNS, which uses both UDP and TCP.

Firewall Options

The **Firewall options** page allows us to enable and disable responses to **ICMP (Internet Control Message Protocol)** **echo** (ping) requests to various interfaces on the IPCop box. Generally it is considered to be a good practice to disable any unnecessary traffic, although ping can be particularly useful when testing, and it is a quite common omission among firewall rules to allow this traffic.

Although not a major issue pertaining to this option, since it only allows ICMP responses to be sent from the IPCop host, there are major reasons to disallow ICMP traffic in environments strict about outgoing traffic. It is possible to tunnel IP traffic (i.e. all connections made via TCP, UDP, and ICMP, including web access, DNS, port scans, and any other type of TCP/IP network activity) over ICMP.

This can lead to a situation in which, using an airport or coffee shop network, a rogue user can access the Internet without paying (since such pre-authentication or payment systems often allow DNS and ICMP traffic to traverse the firewall they have in place), or in a business, an employee can circumvent the firewall policy to gain access to unauthorized resources and sites.

See `http://thomer.com/icmptx/` for more details on tunneling IP over ICMP.

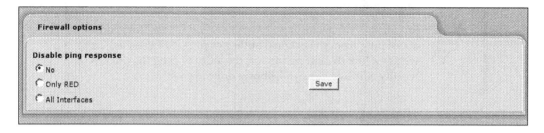

Network Troubleshooting with Ping

Of the three protocols running on top of IP, which constitute the **TCP/IP stack** in common usage on the Internet (TCP, UDP, and ICMP) ICMP is often the most overlooked. ICMP can be viewed as a sort of management channel—ICMP is primarily used for sending error messages and other pieces of information that are used to diagnose problems and handle data.

Ping actually uses the ICMP `echo request` and `echo reply` messages, and the first utility called ping was written in 1983. The way this works is sometimes equated to **SONAR**—an initiating host sends an *echo request* message, usually to a specific host by IP address. The receiving host then replies with an *echo reply* message, and the initiating computer calculates the round trip time, which it displays in milliseconds (ms).

This provides a good, quick test of:

- Connectivity (whether the other host replies)
- Network latency (the length of time taken)
- Network reliability (leaving the `ping` command running, with the `-t` flag in Windows or by default with many other implementations of ping, is often a good way to detect sudden spikes in network usage or latency, or losses of connectivity).

More recently, many hosts on the Internet have started firewalling ICMP traffic of this sort, not responding to `echo request` packets. In some instances, this may be to reduce bandwidth usage, while in others administrators may have blocked it for security reasons. Microsoft (`www.microsoft.com`) is one example of a high profile site that drops ping requests—Google (`www.google.com`) is an example of one that doesn't.

More about Ping

See `http://ftp.arl.mil/~mike/ping.html` for more about ping from the original author of ping, Mike Muuss, as well as a link to (and picture of) the story of ping the duck, a worthy addition to any IT library or bookshelf!

Summary

We have been through the mainstay of IPCop configuration in the web interface, and should by this point have a solid understanding of how we can employ the various options IPCop makes available to us to administer, troubleshoot, and monitor our IPCop firewall in a variety of different scenarios.

6
Intrusion Detection with IPCop

Now that we have a working firewall with most of the basic features set up, we are feeling pretty secure. Surely no malicious intruder could get past these defenses on our network. What if they did though? How would we know? What would we do?

These are questions that an **Intrusion Detection System** (**IDS**) tries to answer; it detects when things don't go entirely to plan in regards to network security and logs any suspicious activity that it recognizes, so that we can effectively deal with a security incident.

Introduction to IDS

There are a variety of Intrusion Detection Systems in the market ranging from the enterprise-level managed-network monitoring solution to a simple on-the-host logging system. There is also a distinction between an **Intrusion Prevention System** (**IPS**) and an IDS. An IPS goes one better than the IDS and attempts to block an attack in progress whereas the IDS attempts to log the attack and optionally notify a responsible party to employ an incident response plan.

IDSs can be further categorized as **NIDS** or **HIDS**, the difference being that the former watches the *network* and the latter monitors the *host*. This is important when choosing an IDS as we have to be sure of what exactly we are monitoring.

For example, many administrators won't employ a HIDS on Windows or Unix boxes due to their built-in abilities to log extensively (event logs/syslog), and therefore prefer to monitor the traffic on the network for signs of malicious behavior. This can also be more reliable than host monitoring as it's hard to trust the logs of a compromised host.

In the case of IPCop what we have is a built-in NIDS on our firewall, pre-configured and ready to use with the absolute minimal configuration, the **Snort** intrusion detection system.

Introduction to Snort

Snort is the IDS included with IPCop, and is one of the best-known and commonly used **sniffers** available today and used by networks large and small the world over. It has continually updated signatures for a massive number of vulnerabilities, a massive user base, commercial support, and excellent documentation available online as well as in print. Snort was initially developed by Martin Roesch in the late 1990's and was destined to be a sniffer and possibly a little more, hence the name Snort.

Initially as a sniffer Snort was quite good and was linked to its slightly older relative TCPDUMP. Eventually Snort was expanded and become known as more of a NIDS than a sniffer (many of Snort's users are unaware of its sniffing capabilities and use it purely as an IDS).

As Snort became very popular, Martin Roesch decided to start a company based on Snort to offer security services based on the expertise that he had as a Snort developer. This led to the creation of Sourcefire (`http://www.sourcefire.com`). Sourcefire now offers commercial support and other services based on Snort. Though it also employs full time developers for Snort, it still remains an open-source product, and hence can be provided with IPCop. The IPCop developers add to this a pre-configured Snort system with very easy-to-use and simple management options in the IPCop interface.

Do We Need an IDS?

The need of an IDS depends entirely on the network and what we want to do. Generally I'd say that we need it, unless we can think of a good reason not to have it.

The added benefit of an IDS is that we can see what is passing through our network and attempt to isolate any traffic that appears malicious. This is important as it's a function many firewalls lack (except those with layer-seven support, which are termed application-layer firewalls). Since firewalls work at the lower layers of network communication their filtering rules are generally limited to IP addresses, ports, time of day, and only a few other criteria. If we have a firewall that isn't looking into the payload of a packet and only making decisions based on packet headers, it's far from inconceivable to say that these devices may allow some malicious traffic to pass. The role of our IDS is to do deep inspection of these packets looking at the data contained within and make decisions such as: "Does this look like the Code Red worm?", "Is this an attempt at a buffer overflow in our sendmail server?", or "Has one of our users just been exploited by the latest 0-day WMF exploit?". It's quite valuable for an administrator to be notified of any packets that throw up these warning signs in the IDS, as we can then use this information to look further into the status of our network to see if we have a major issue to contend with, although often these warnings are false alarms. We can think of an IDS as an early warning system that something might be going on that requires our attention. In an attempt to protect our network, this is very valuable information to have!

Layer-7 Filtering (Application Layer)

There are options for IPCop that provide filtering at this layer, but they are not provided by default and require the installation of third-party add-ons.

How Does an IDS Work?

NIDS in general, and Snort specifically, are run on devices that have the ability to monitor as much of the network as possible, generally on or near a gateway device, (as in the case of IPCop) or on some sort of monitoring port on a switch (SPAN/ Mirror ports). The NIDS then sets up the network card or cards on the device to work in **promiscuous mode** meaning they will pass packets up through the network stack whether or not they are destined for the machine. This is important as a NIDS will often be monitoring machines other than itself. The NIDS on the host will then take these packets and have a look at the data payload (and sometimes the headers as well) to see if it notices anything malicious. This may sound like artificial intelligence as the NIDS just sits there thinking to itself about packets passing by; it's actually quite a lot simpler than that!

Every day exploits, viruses, worms, spyware, and other malicious software generate network traffic, and this traffic often has patterns specific to the piece of software in use, a specific string in an exploit, specific hosts it contacts, and specific options in the TCP/IP headers. There are many people watching their networks and as they notice something that looks strange they document it and generally seek advice from their peers to see if anyone notices something similar. Quite shortly afterwards, if malicious activity is detected, someone will write a signature for their favorite IDS and in many cases for a few IDSs all at once. Based on these signatures the IDS detection engine will decide whether to flag a packet as possibly malicious. These are rarely 100% accurate as they can and will provide false positives or negatives. This detection is designed as an extra layer of defense and cannot say for sure that a network has or has not been compromised. What can be done is alerting of an administrator that something is up. Snort on an IPCop box is placed in an excellent position to alert on any malicious behavior attempting to pass through the firewall to protected interfaces—or even between protected interfaces.

Using Snort with IPCop

Setting up Snort with IPCop is a very straightforward process. SourceFire require users to register if they want to download updated signatures. We really do want to have updated rules, and so we should ensure we register with SourceFire. This can be done by following the instruction on the following screen for registering on the Snort website and generating an Oink code.

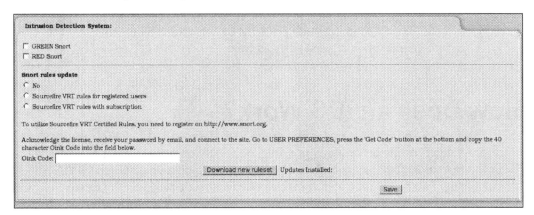

Once registered, we fill in the form on the previous screen. We select each interface we want to monitor by marking the corresponding checkbox. The author's preference is to monitor all interfaces at this point and filter later when monitoring the logs. We should also choose **SourceFire VRT rules for registered users** unless we have a paid for subscription that allows us access to the subscription rules. Then we enter our **Oink Code** as obtained from the Snort website. We can now download the most up-to-date rules. That's it! We have now, by filling in a very simple form, configured a NIDS for our network. Now surely we are secure!

Monitoring the Logs

An intrusion detection system on its own isn't any good whatsoever; it needs a set of eyes to look over the logs and take action or some sort of automated notification system. IPCop's web interface provides a primitive first look at what is going on in the network.

This can be found under the **Logs IDS Logs** menu option as shown in the following figure:

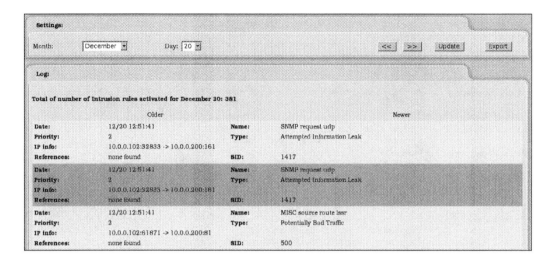

The log screen defaults to today's date and gives us some interesting information. Today on December 20th 381 rules were activated, meaning that Snort noticed 381 possible attacks on the network. This number is abnormally high as the data was generated artificially by the author, but generally you would expect to see a few rules activated per day depending on the size of your network. Home users should expect to see a lot of port scans and automated worm attacks for example. If we take a closer look at one of the rules, we can see what Snort has shown us in the logs.

Date:12/20 12:51:41 Name:SNMP request udp

Priority:2 Type:Attempted Information Leak

IP info: 10.0.0.102:32833 -> 10.0.0.200:161

References: none found SID: 1417

We can see that someone from the computer at IP address **10.0.0.102** attempted to gain information on our network using a **UDP**-based **SNMP** request from port **32833** on the attacker to port **161** on **10.0.0.200**. We also have a **SID** value of **1417**. This is good basic information to let us know what is going on. We can see who, what, where, and when—which are very important for intrusion detection. The only value we don't have an obvious explanation for here is the SID.

The SID is the the Snort Signature ID and the number itself is a link to the online database of SIDs, which contains more information about this event.

GEN:SID	1:634
Message	Sorry, no such sid-gen (1:634)
Summary	This event is generated when a scan is detected.
Impact	Information gathering.
Detailed Information	This event indicates that an attempt has been made to scan a host.
	This may be the prelude to an attack. Scanners are used to ascertain which ports a host may be listening on, whether or not the ports are filtered by a firewall and if the host is vulnerable to a particular exploit.
Affected Systems	Any host.
Attack Scenarios	An attacker can determine if ports 21 and 20 are being used for FTP. Then the attacker might find out that the FTP service is vulnerable to a particular attack and is then able to compromise the host.
Ease of Attack	Simple.
False Positives	A scanner may be used in a security audit. If you think this rule has a false positives, please help fill it out.
False Negatives	None Known. If you think this rule has a false negatives, please help fill it out.
Corrective Action	Determine whether or not the scan was legitimate then look for other events concerning the attacking IP address.
	Check the host for signs of compromise.
Contributors	Sourcefire Vulnerability Research Team Brian Caswell <bmc@sourcefire.com> Nigel Houghton <nigel.houghton@sourcefire.com>
Additional References	

This gives us a lot of information and lets us narrow down exactly what happened in this case. In the false positives section we can see that this event can occur when the system is scanned by security scanning software, which in this case is entirely correct, as the author scanned the IPCop box with OpenVAS, (`http://www.openvas.org`) an open-source vulnerability scanner.

OpenVAS

OpenVAS is a fork of the Nessus security scanner, now being developed as a separate project in order to give an alternative to the latest non-GPL version of Nessus.

Priority

Another very important field is the priority, which in this case is **2**. Snort has the following three levels by default:

- Level 1:
    - Executable code detected
    - Attempt or success in gaining administrative privilege
    - Trojan signatures

- Level 2:
  - ° Attempted/Successful Denial of Service
  - ° Attempted/Successful Information Leak
  - ° Unusual client port connection

- Level 3:
  - ° Port Scanning
  - ° Suspicious string detection

Whenever an attack is detected, the rule it matches has a priority level that is referenced in order to give the event its priority number. These numbers are part of the rule and can be modified if necessary by manually altering the Snort rules. Manual alteration of Snort's configuration will not be covered here; however, there are many books and a lot of online documentation available on the subject of Snort.

Log Analysis Options

Snort, being such a well-used project, has a variety of analysis products available. We will take a quick look at some of the most commonly used products and the features they provide. The IPCop logging system is not entirely adequate for most analysis, and definitely cannot be used to provide reports, which are commonly required whenever there is an intrusion attempt. Many projects have been created in order to analyze and report on these logs. In order to use these tools you may have to configure IPCop to log to a remote syslog server or in some cases you can install and add on to IPCop.

Perl Scripts

One of the easiest install-and-use products for Snort log analysis is the excellent SnortALog. It offers some excellent features, the most useful being the abilities it has for report generation—you can have reports in ASCII, PDF, or HTML format with images represented as GIF, PNG, or JPEG. This makes for excellent reporting as you can be provided with a variety of graphs and statistics that can then be used in presentations or other reports, on the security status of the network. SnortALog works with all output options available with Snort and has an easy-to-use GUI for generating reports. There is also the option of SnortSnarf, which offers features similar to those of SnortALog; however SnortALog is fairly easy to use, and apparently SnortSnarf is no longer being developed. SnortALog also provides more report options and has a more polished look.

ACID and BASE

There are also some more full-featured and complicated systems that can be used for monitoring and analyzing Snort logs. **ACID** for example is PHP-based, requires the use of a web server, and provides real-time monitoring and statistics of the Snort log. Moreover with the statistics generated with the above PERL scripts, you have very powerful options for further analysis. For example, you can query quite extensively to be provided with only the events of most interest for your current analysis, you can view the packet contents that generated the event, and closely analyze the packet data to fully determine the extent of the attack and whether it was a false positive. **BASE** is an alternative (forked from ACID) to ACID, provides similar features, and it is worth comparing the two to find the product preferred for our monitoring of the intrusion detection system.

What to Do Next?

Once you have identified that an incident has occurred, it is important to quickly act on the incident. Although Snort itself provides nothing more than a few ideas on looking further at a specific event, it's the responsibility of the administrator to decide how to handle an event.

In a smaller network a formalized incident response plan isn't always necessary, but it does help in maintaining system security if we have an idea of what to do if subjected to a specific attack. Some good examples would be port scans, denial of service, and exploitation attempts. We can then decide on things like:

- Do we want to report these?
- Do we want to analyze other protection systems if they occur?
- Do we have to notify someone?

Answering a few basic questions like these as you set up your IDS gives the IDS much more value as it becomes part of a valid plan for network protection.

Summary

In this chapter we have covered the basics of what an IDS is, how it works, how to use Snort with IPCop, and additional tools for use with Snort.

At this point we have knowledge of network protection, network monitoring, and at least a basic idea of what we would do if an attack attempt occurs. This puts us in a good situation on our network and ensures we are fully aware of what is going on. As mentioned in the introduction to this chapter, an IDS is supposed to give us a basic overview of the security status of the network—are we being attacked, where is it coming from, and what are the targets.

Armed with this information we can effectively increase the security of our network. Using an automated tool such as this means it is much easier for us to monitor these activities daily and ensure that we are always aware of our surroundings. Knowing how our network functions and what sort of data passes through it daily is an important measure in spotting network intrusions. We cannot be aware that something is going wrong if we don't have a baseline to compare this against; constantly monitoring our IDS gives us that baseline.

7
Virtual Private Networks

As discussed in earlier chapters, many of the technologies underpinning the way in which networking works were designed with considerations quite different to those facing IT professionals and computer users today. Among the most salient of these are concerns about security.

Remote access, another principal concern among IT Professionals, is the practice of allowing employees, contractors, clients, and suppliers to access resources and services over a Wide Area Network or the Internet. This practice, since it necessarily involves not only connecting a company's internal network to the Internet but also allowing traffic from the Internet to gain access to the internal network, brings with it inherent security risks. Some of them stem from the ability that remote access systems give to an attacker to probe and attack the network, while some of them stem from the fact that conventionally, information is passed over the Internet in plain text with no form of tamper protection.

The implication of this last concern is that if we use a conventional protocol such as HTTP or NFS to access our information or give access to our information to others over the Internet, anyone with the right degree of access (i.e. anyone with physical or logical access to our network infrastructure—switches, routers, hubs, firewalls, anywhere between us and our destination) can intercept, read, copy, or alter our information in transit.

Rather than simply open up services such as HTTP servers, mail servers, file servers, and terminal services or VNC servers to the Internet, then, it has become a growing practice to secure these services behind a **VPN**, or **Virtual Private Network.**

What is a VPN?

As the name implies, a VPN is a *network* that is *virtual*. That is to say, unlike the local network at a business or small office that consists of, in some cases, many thousands of yards of cabling and many network devices, a *virtual* network contains no substance at all — in fact, it exists on top of existing networks. It is also private, which means in this case that it is both *encrypted* (so that third parties cannot see what we are sending and receiving) and *authenticated* (we need to identify ourselves, generally with a password, in order to use it).

Consider a scenario involving a small company with a small number of sales employees who routinely work from different parts of the country (or even the world). The sales staff needs to regularly synchronize its sales information with the other sales employees, both out of the office and in the office, and it needs to send and receive email and access other types of company information. These services have, until now, been accessible only behind our firewall.

Using a Virtual Private Network, a sales employee connects a laptop to the wireless network in the hotel he or she is staying in, providing internet access using the wireless adapter in his or her computer. Once connected to the Internet via Wi-Fi, he or she connects to the corporate VPN, and the VPN client software establishes a secure connection to the corporate VPN server. A new, virtual, network interface appears on the laptop, with an IP address allocated to the sales employee's laptop corresponding to the internal segment of the corporate network.

Traffic destined for the internal network can now go via this network interface. Traffic through this interface is encapsulated by the VPN client software and sent via the encrypted VPN link — where it is un-encapsulated at the other end by the VPN server and routed into the internal network. The Head of Sales, at his or her desk within the corporate network at head office, can see the sales employee's laptop on the network as if it were physically plugged into the network, albeit with slightly slower access!

This is a gross oversimplification of, technically, how VPN software actually works — but it gives a good general idea of how the process occurs at a high level. Network-aware applications (such as an email client, FTP client, or Samba client) can access resources on the internal network without being aware of the network link by simply making the same connections they have done before — the VPN software and drivers handle the encapsulation and un-encapsulation. VPNs are increasingly used by companies for scenarios very similar to the one above, using a variety of technologies including **IP Security (IPSec)**, **Layer Two Tunneling Protocol (L2TP)**, **Point To Point Tunneling Protocol (PPTP)**, SSH, SSL, and several proprietary protocols such as that used by the proprietary VPN service Hamachi.

In addition to giving access to another network, some VPN systems recently set up, such as that offered by Hamachi or the VPN service that comes as part of the Google Wi-Fi service, simply serve to offer some guarantee of privacy when using untrusted network connections (particularly wireless network connections in public places, which are typically unencrypted and non-secure).

> **Proprietary Internet-Based VPN Services**
>
> Hamachi's VPN service (`http://www.hamachi.cc/`) is one example of a growing breed of internet-based VPN services seeking only to offer privacy (i.e. the user does not gain access to any *extra* resources not available to the Internet at large, unlike our sales employee and his or her corporate VPN) to users on untrusted network connections such as Wi-Fi networks.
>
> In such situations, traffic is tunneled to the servers owned by the proprietors of the VPN connection, and the *extra* privacy is provided by the assumption that these proprietors (such as Hamachi) are less likely to try to intercept your information than your fellow users of the untrusted network you are connected via (possibly with a policy backing this up).

IPSec

Although many VPN protocols are in common deployment (both PPTP and L2TP being in wide deployment due to their use as part of the Windows family of products), IPSec is the most independent, standardized solution, and is incorporated into most VPN solutions in one form or another.

Most IPSec-capable devices will form tunnels with other such devices, although this is not guaranteed—lower-end devices such as SOHO routers in particular with such functionality are often extremely hard to configure and troubleshoot, and typically have poor support from the manufacturer for the IPSec functionality. Although IPSec should be interoperable, it can often save a lot of pain to use the same device at both ends! It is also worth noting while on the topic of interoperability that IPSec only supports **Main Mode** IPSec, and not **Aggressive Mode** IPSec.

PPTP and L2TP

PPTP was originally designed by Cisco and later licensed by Microsoft as a VPN protocol for Windows Dial-Up Networking (in fact, the first VPN protocol supported natively in Windows). Traffic is authenticated using **MicroSoft Challenge-Handshake Authentication Protocol v2 (MS-CHAPv2)** or **Extensible Authentication Protocol-Transport Layer Security (EAP-TLS)** (with certificates), and encrypted using **MPPE (RSA RC4)**. Although PPTP is strengthened by certificates and is significantly less complex than IPSec, without certificates it is still weaker than IPSec, and suffers from less widescale implementation.

L2TP is an evolutionary progression of both Cisco's **Layer 2 Forwarding (L2F)** and PPTP. It does not implement authentication or encryption, and so it is generally employed in conjunction with IPSec in order to form a VPN. Due to the use of IPSec, an L2TP/IPSec VPN is more secure than one using PPTP, and the potential exists to use higher-grade encryption.

IPSec itself has a broader scope than simply being used for VPNs, and is a mandatory part of the **Internet Protocol version 6 (IPv6)** specification. It was originally conceived with two deployment scenarios in mind:

- **Tunnel Mode**: IPSec in tunnel mode is designed, as in the previous scenario, to *tunnel* traffic from more than one host (or an entire network or networks) to another host or set of networks with endpoints being used to encapsulate and de-encapsulate traffic before and after it traverses an intermediary network, generally the Internet.

- **Transport Mode**: IPSec in transport mode is designed to secure IP communications in general. This deployment, although possible over the Internet, is generally deployed to protect LAN segments, either in mission-critical scenarios in which communication between particular hosts must be encrypted such as a web and database server, or to protect an entire network. Such a system may be employed as part of a distributed firewalling policy — by configuring all hosts on a network to talk to each other only using IPSec, any unauthorized host connecting to the network is unable to directly connect to other hosts, effectively isolating that host at a certain layer of the network.

Such a setup is employed by Microsoft as part of its Server and Domain Isolation (see http://www.microsoft.com/technet/itsolutions/network/sd-iso/default.mspx for more information on logical isolation using

IPSec, in this case on the Windows platform) security best practice, and forms a part of both the **Network Access Protection** (**NAP**) and **Network Access Quarantine Control** (**NAQC**) frameworks.

As we can see, IPSec is a complex topic, and can be employed to do many things. For the scope of this chapter, however, all we need to know is that IPSec may be used to secure IP traffic, and that in this scenario, IPCop utilizes IPSec as part of a VPN system to allow remote clients to appear as if they were virtually plugged into the internal network via a secure, encrypted tunnel over the Internet, and one or more networks (such as a client's internal network or a hotel wireless network). We may also use IPSec to link two IPCop firewalls (or an IPCop firewall and another IPSec-capable router or firewall) in order to form a *virtual* site-to-site network. The following links provide excellent starting points to learn more about IPSec:

- `http://www.packtpub.com/openswan/book`: The Openswan book, written by the developers of Openswan itself

- `http://www.openswan.org/docs/`: The Openswan documentation

- `http://en.wikipedia.org/wiki/IPSec`: Wikipedia article on IPSec

A Little More about Deploying IPSec

A basic understanding of IPSec is important to anyone wishing to adequately set up, manage, maintain, or support a network utilizing IPSec as part of a site-to-site deployment.

Even solutions that are less *hands on* than IPCop, such as commercial firewalls with site-to-site VPN solutions designed to be simple to deploy, frequently require advanced debugging, which in turn requires an in-depth knowledge of the protocols they use. Commercial firewalling packages with VPN support such as Microsoft's ISA Server, Checkpoint, Borderware, or any firewall appliance from a small VPN router all the way through enterprise-grade firewalls are frequently difficult to troubleshoot.

Appliances in particular, due to their use in many instances of customized free IPSec software, are difficult to troubleshoot because of their similarities to other IPSec packages but with modifications made by the OEM vendor. Wikipedia at the time of writing lists nine different vendors of IPSec software.

For all of these reasons (and good old fashioned curiosity), you hopefully have some idea as to why you might (or might not!) want to learn about IPSec.

We can set up IPSec in IPCop in two ways: one of these is referred to as IPSec with a **Pre-shared key**; a pre-shared key is like a password known to both endpoints of the connection. Although simple to set up, this is less secure than the second of the two ways, which relies on certificates issued by a Certificate Authority (CA).

Pre-Shared Keys versus Certificates

A PSK is less secure than certificate because it is an inherently weaker security mechanism. A pre-shared key is generally (like passwords) chosen because it is memorable to a human, and therefore it is infinitely easier to crack by brute force than a certificate, which constitutes a highly random set of characters and necessitates knowledge both of the public and private key portions in order to cause a breach of security.

Certificates may be issued by a CA such as Verisign, Thawte, or CAcert.org, or you may set up your own CA (either solely for the purpose of generating these certificates or as part of a larger PKI system) in order to do this. You do not have to pay money for this, and it does not have to be a (very) painful experience.

Configuring your own CA

If you run Windows Server with Active Directory, you probably already have the infrastructure and software in place for a flexible, secure PKI system with your own CA. There is excellent guidance on Microsoft TechNet about this:

```
http://www.microsoft.com/windowsserver2003/
technologies/pki/default.mspx
```

If you are using another operating system, or would prefer to separate your PKI environment from your Windows infrastructure, onlamp.com has a good primer on this at the following URL:

```
http://www.onlamp.com/pub/a/
onlamp/2003/02/06/linuxhacks.html
```

Running your own CA, especially if you start to rely on it for tasks such as IPSec and file encryption, is an extremely important role in any business, one which (if broken) can cause large headaches for productivity, and (if compromised) can potentially do a lot of damage. You are very well advised to read up on best practice for Certificate Authorities if you do decide to take this step, and heed some of the words of wisdom offered by those who are experts in the area.

> The Microsoft guidance, although Windows-specific, has
> excellent guidelines with regard to CA best practice, and
> many of the recommendations to do with CA location and
> management, and the use of smartcards and HSMs, apply
> irrespective of the platform and OS you choose to run your
> CA on. At the very least, if you do not have a Windows
> infrastructure, it is worth seeing how *the other side* does it
> (and if its implementation has any merit) before setting such
> an infrastructure up yourself.

Prerequisites for a Successful VPN

For a site-to-site VPN, the IPSec setup process can also be somewhat confusing due
to the terminology. For this reason, it is particularly important to write down all of
the information required to set up the VPN before you try to set it up. The author
would even go so far as to suggest the use of an easy-to-understand form such as the
one displayed on a following page.

A significant majority of problems with VPN setups (many of which are frustrating
and take a lot of time) are caused by misconfigurations and non-matching settings.
Taking a few extra minutes to formulate your deployment plan and clearly marking
out your settings on a piece of paper will save you valuable time and sanity.

Our prerequisites are:

A Reliable Network

As VPN connections are made over an intermediary network such as the Internet,
their success and stability rely upon the reliability of the intermediary network.
VPNs introduce more overhead to the network, and any latency or low bandwidth
will therefore be (marginally) amplified over the VPN.

Two Endpoints Attached to the Internet Running IPSec Software

We require IPSec software running on both endpoints in order to make a site-to-site
VPN work!

Static Red IP Addresses for Both Endpoints or Dynamic DNS Hostnames

Without these we have no way to establish a connection consistently. Although
rare, some ISPs allocate addresses in the RFC1918 range to clients—that is to say,
192.168.0.0/16, 10.0.0.0/8, and 172.16.0.0/12. Although it is unlikely that you don't,
check you have a real IP address first!

Non-Overlapping Internal Address Spaces

Without non-overlapping address ranges, we cannot route traffic from one site to the other.

As you may have understood from the earlier chapter on networking, routes and routing are very important in the delivery of data from one network subnet to another. When a computer tries to connect to another computer — for instance, to connect to an SSH server on 192.0.2.33 — the operating system first checks to ascertain whether this IP address is local. If our computer has the IP address 192.0.22.99 with the subnet mask of 255.255.255.0, the computer performs a calculation using the IP address and netmask in binary to discover which portion of the IP address is the *network* portion, and which is the *host* portion. In this instance, the first three octets of the IP address (192, 0, and 22) are the network portion, while the fourth (and last) octet is the host portion.

Seeing that the network portion of the 192.0.2.33 address (192.0.2) does not match the network portion of the IP address of the computer making the connection (192.0.22), the computer cannot connect to the destination directly via a switch or hub, and therefore has to pass data to a router to route data either directly to the destination or to the destination via one or more routers.

The routing table contains a list of entries with networks corresponding to IP addresses through which these subnets are reached. As the client computer must connect to *a* router in order to send *any* data to a non-local machine, every router IP address listed in the routing table *must* be in the same subnet as the IP address assigned to the network card(s) in the client machine. Generally speaking, client computers will tend to have only one network card with only one (important) route — that of the default router. This is the router to which the client computer will pass traffic to if there are no other, higher entries in the routing table, and is generally where most traffic goes.

You can display the output of your routing table in most Linux distributions using the `ip route list` command, and in Linux and most Unix distributions, the `route` command with no parameters. In Windows using the `route print` command will display the routing table.

In a VPN configuration, our hosts must know which subnet is at the other end of the VPN connection, and which subnet is local. Use of overlapping IP ranges will therefore break VPNs — if we have a network using the 192.168.0.1/24 (or 192.168.0.1 with a subnet mask of 255.255.255.0) address range, and have a VPN configured with a network also using the 192.168.0.1/24 address range, our computer or VPN router will be unable to route packets from one range to another, as it will not know in *which* 192.168.0.1/24 address range the host 192.168.0.22 computer is.

Address space should be planned, and if you anticipate your network ever needing access to VPNs or site-to-site VPNs, you should pick a non-default private IP address range (such as somewhere in the 10.0.0.0/8, (10.0.0.1 to 10.255.255.255) range, or a non-standard 192.168.0.0/16 subnet, (such as 192.168.130.0/24) in order to make your life easier further down the line.

Time and Patience

The *left* and *right* terminology used by IPCop can be slightly confusing—the best advice that one can give on this front is to pick one site as *left*, and the other as *right*. The form overleaf demonstrates this—one site is clearly marked **L** and one **R**. To put this differently, *configure both ends of the VPN identically*!

IP Addresses

These examples use *external* addresses in the 172.16.0.0/12 address range—your actual Red *external* addresses, if you configure a VPN operating over the Internet, will be *public* addresses assigned by your ISP.

For the purpose of this chapter, we will consider the following net-to-net configuration between two IPCop firewalls in physically separate locations, Cambridge and Oxford. For the purpose of this example, these two hosts are to be considered to be set up IPCop firewalls in the Red-Green configuration, with internet connections that have fixed IP addresses.

LEFT HAND SITE		Site Name: ____Cambridge_____
RED (External) IP	____172.16.12.19	Gateway (Internal) IP ___192.168.0.10__
		Internal Network __192.168.0.0/24_
Pre-Shared Key: _____"Don't talk to strangers!"_____		

RIGHT HAND SITE		Site Name: ____Oxford_____
RED (External) IP	____172.16.22.19	Gateway (Internal) IP __192.168.1.1____
		Internal Network __192.168.1.0/24_
Pre-Shared Key: _____"£agh@;323lkj$%=sdf9SD-+"_____		

The following page contains a blank version of these forms so that you can, if you wish, use these forms for your own environment.

LEFT HAND SITE   **Site Name:** _____

RED (External) IP   _____   Gateway (Internal) IP   _____

Internal Network   _____

Pre-Shared Key: _____

NOTES:

RIGHT HAND SITE   **Site Name:** _____

RED (External) IP   _____   Gateway (Internal) IP   _____

Internal Network   _____

Pre-Shared Key: _____

NOTES:

First of all, on the Cambridge firewall, we configure the global settings with the Red IP:

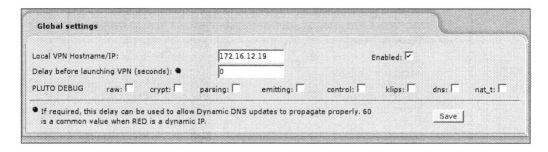

Next, we add a new VPN and select the **Net-to-Net Virtual Private Network**:

Next, we enter the VPN configuration settings into the dialog:

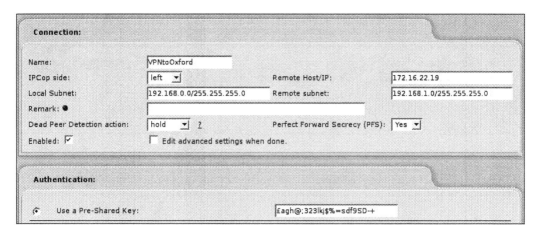

> **Additional IPSec Settings**
>
> **Perfect Forward Secrecy (PFS)** and **Dead Peer Detection (DPD)** are two additional settings you may wish to consider enabling. Both require support at both ends of the VPN tunnel, but respectively improve security and effective service provision.
>
>
>
> PFS ensures that in the event that a key used to encrypt data over the VPN is broken, data encrypted using other keys is not also at risk—the property of Perfect Forward Secrecy in cryptography compartmentalizes data compromise in the event that cryptography is ever broken, causing an attacker to have to break *every* key used in the lifetime of a session to intercept or decrypt all of the session's data, rather than being able to break one key and access all of the session's data.
>
> DPD uses **Internet Key Exchange (IKE)**, to query the IPSec partner to ensure that it is still alive. This ensures that your IPSec endpoint accurately knows the state of the session, since it will detect faults and close the connection (and therefore re-establish the session, if possible) more speedily.

Next, we add the VPN and verify that it appears in the main **VPN** dialog:

Once we configure an identical VPN (with appropriate configuration information) on the Oxford IPCop host (as the 'right' side), our VPN should be functional.

Verifying Connectivity

In recent iterations of IPCop, there is a clear indicator on the VPN page indicating the status of the VPN. Our first port of call after that, however, is the network status screen, where we should see an **UP** VPN interface of the type *ipsecX*, where X is a number (iterating up from 0 for each VPN we configure).

We should also check the routing table using either the `route` command or the `netstat` command with the `r` flag (`netstat -nr`) for the presence of routes to the subnet on the other side of the VPN tunnel. If all appears good, we can try pinging a host within the private subnet on the remote side.

Generally, VPN problems are down to configuration issues, many of which can be avoided by paying careful attention to the pre-requisites for a sensible VPN—some examples of these are that parameters don't match, subnets overlap, or there is a network configuration issue. It is always worth resetting the existing VPN configuration before trying afresh, and if in doubt, a second pair of eyes often helps spot the mistakes that you've missed.

If you're absolutely positive that your configuration matches, and your networks are properly configured, it's possible that you have an interoperability issue. Different devices supporting IPSec quite frequently don't work together as expected, and sometimes don't work at all. SOHO and embedded devices with modified versions of the Openswan IPSec stack quite frequently exhibit very strange behavior when talking to *normal* Openswan installations and other IPSec stacks. It is, in fact, quite frequent for cheap routers supporting IPSec to only talk to other routers with identical model numbers and identical firmware versions, and not even to talk to other routers from the same vendor. This is a fairly prickly area, and isn't often a lot of fun. If in doubt, an IPSec stack you have control over (such as IPCop's), or a well-supported stack (such as the one that you might find on a Cisco router under support) is often worth the extra expense or effort.

Although not covered by our setup here, which used static addresses for the Red interfaces, the IPCop firewall does allow the use of *dynamic* DNS names (as covered in the management chapter) for VPNs. As the VPN configuration page indicates, it can take a short period of time for these updates to happen after the IPCop machine boots up; so if your system uses dynamic DNS and IPSec, you may want to configure the *delay* before bringing up VPNs of 60 seconds (or more) in order to prevent the VPN from failing. This is also worth bearing in mind if failures consistently happen in the first few minutes of the host being booted up!

Host-to-Net Connections Using Pre-Shared Keys

Our procedure for host-to-net, or road warrior, connections is very similar to that of the net-to-net configuration. We first select the appropriate VPN type in the **Add** dialog:

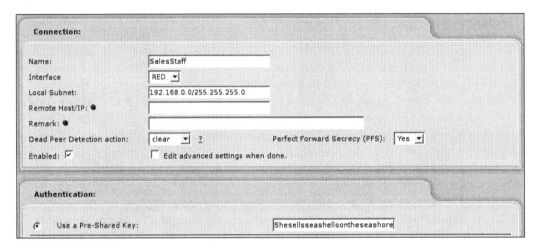

Then, we configure the VPN with appropriate parameters:

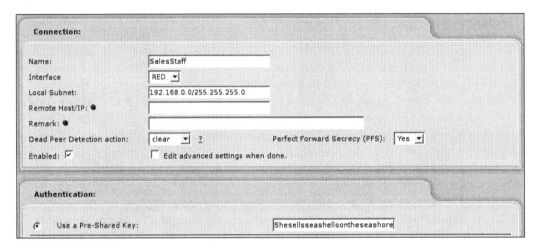

It is worth noting that you are restricted to one host-to-net connection with a PSK.

Host-to-Net Connections Using Certificates

Certificate-based VPNs are substantially more complex to configure than Pre-Shared Keys, but also increase the level of security offered by the VPN significantly.

A Brief Explanation of Certificates and X.509

Note that this book does *not* explain X.509, certificates, or cryptography thoroughly — the information here is designed to give you some idea in what context IPSec functions such that you understand what it is doing — but further, to give you just enough information to understand what you *don't* know and can read about yourself if you consider it important.

These are very complex topics, and are well worth spending hours or even days reading about if this is the technology that you use. Wikipedia, which has comprehensive articles on almost all of the technical terms mentioned here, while not authoritative, generally serves as an excellent pointer in the right direction(s), and frequently has excellent content.

Certificates in this context are X.509 certificates, which have their origins in X.500, which is a set of standards for directory services, including the protocol, **Directory Access Protocol (DAP)**, the predecessor to LDAP.

Directory services, broadly speaking, are a set of applications and protocols used to store information about a network, the services it offers, and its users, and commonly include information such as usernames, user profiles, logon information, security information, and many other pieces of application-specific information.

The *directory* in a directory service system is a database that is stored, generally in a central location on directory servers. The database commonly has entries for users, computers, and other objects, with parameters for each object such as *username* or *extension number* in the case of a user.

X.509 certificates are similar to entries in a directory in that they store a number of parameters inside a single file. The parameters stored within an X.509 certificate include several mandatory fields such as a serial number, the subject, the issuer, and information about the key stored in the certificate, as well as having provision for *extensions* used to incorporate additional information into the certificate, and functionality into the X.509 PKI system.

The X.509 system uses Certificate Authorities (CA), which issue and manage these certificates. There is a hierarchy of such CAs, and CAs usually exist at the top of the tree.

If you open a copy of any modern browser, you have incorporated into the browser (or, in Windows, the operating system itself), a certificate store. In Windows this can be accessed via Internet Explorer by clicking on **Tools | Internet Options | Content | Certificates**, which displays a window similar to the following:

The tabs along the top of the window indicate the *type* of certificate being viewed — in this example, the tab selected (which is the default tab) is that of **Personal** certificates, which are certificates issued by a Certificate Authority to a user or computer. These might be used to send signed email using a standard such as **S/MIME**, or to access a VPN using IPSec.

The private key associated with the certificate would in these cases be used either to sign the email in order to verify the sender (or possibly sign the email in addition to encrypting it to another S/MIME user using their public key) or to authenticate to a VPN server.

The right-most tab visible in the previous image is **Trusted Root Certification Authorities**.

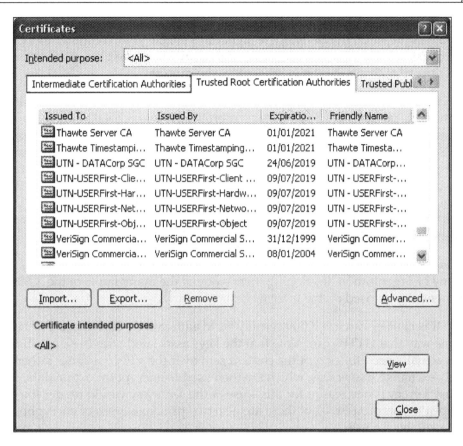

In the same way that I can verify a PGP-signed email sent to me if I have the public key of the person who sent it (mathematically, I can establish that the email was sent by the owner of the corresponding private key in a manner impractical to subvert), I can verify that a certificate was signed by one of the private keys associated with the *root* certificates displayed in the previous image.

Since distributing keys is hard, signing with a root certificate is important because it enables us to put all of our trust in one place. Since we know that (in theory) VeriSign issue certificates to people only after having verified that they are who they say they are, it stands to reason that if we are presented with a secure email certificate for `joebloggs@somecompany.com` signed by Verisign's root certificate, the sender of the email is `joebloggs@somecompany.com` (assuming that we trust both Verisign and somecompany.com's security).

Within the context of online shopping, email, and many other things, this is extremely important! Put briefly, these signatures enable your computer to make decisions about how to handle certificates based on who signed the certificates and whether we trust them and their certificate-issue process.

HTTPS uses X.509 certificates as part of SSL, so when you view a secure website (with the URL prefixed by `https://`), your browser either recognises that the certificate used by SSL is issued by a root Certificate Authority for that address, or that it isn't. In the latter case, the browser will usually pop up an error—this might be because the certificate is issued for a slightly different web address (for instance, if you visit `https://www.gmail.com`, which uses the certificate for a different URL), or because the certificate is self-signed or signed by a root certificate not in your trusted root certificate store (such as CAcert, `www.cacert.org`, or on a device—such as smartphone—without a full set of trusted root certificates).

Root certificates are included in products such as browsers at the discretion of the company or organisation developing them—one of the many faults of the X.509 PKI implementation as used on the Internet.

Back to IPSec; IPSec can use X.509 certificates to authenticate clients in a VPN in the same way that HTTPS can. Note that the keys associated with these certificates are not actually used to encrypt the content sent over the VPN itself, but rather to securely exchange *session keys*, which are then used to encrypt the actual data. Perfect Forward Secrecy is one reason for this—use of the same key would render the entire VPN open to compromise—but there are also two principle types of encryption cipher available for use.

One, commonly used for encrypted email or file encryption, uses public and private keys, and is referred to as an **asymmetric** cipher, whereby a public key is used to encrypt data, which is then in a format only accessible by the holder of the private key. This type of cipher is excellent for use in communications like email, as you can distribute your public key at whim, and users can encrypt information to you offline, anywhere in the world, and send it to you over an untrusted network. Only when you get that information is it decrypted.

The other, **symmetric** ciphers, only use one key—the same key to encrypt and decrypt. Due to the mathematics involved, these ciphers are a lot faster to encrypt and decrypt, but because of the single key used, less practical—key distribution becomes a problem, as in an environment with a large number of people, a very large number of keys are required in order to allow everyone to securely communicate with everyone else—one key per person, in fact, for every other person in the group!

Due to the practicalities of using asymmetric ciphers on a fast stream of data, communications such as IPSec and SSH generate symmetric keys (using ciphers such as RC4, AES, and blowfish) for transmitting data, and then use asymmetric keys (using ciphers such as RSA) to exchange the keys used for this transmission before the session is fully established.

Certificates with IPSec in IPCop

Version 1.4.0 of IPCop not only contains support for certificate-based IPSec tunnels, but also a built-in CA in order to avoid the hassle of configuring your own CA or the expense of buying certificates from a third-party CA!

Our first step in configuring a certificate-based IPSec VPN, therefore, is in the VPN **Certificate Authorities** window. By default in IPCop, this will list both **Root Certificate** and **Host Certificate** as **Not present**.

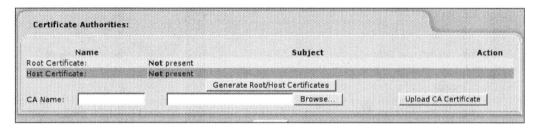

If we are using an existing root CA (or configuring a site-to-site VPN), we need to upload certificate files using the **Upload CA Certificate** button, but for a road warrior configuration (or prior to uploading the certificate files from another firewall), we first need to enter a name for the CA into the **CA Name** field, and when this is done, start the process of generating our own root CA and host certificate, by clicking on **Generate Root/Host Certificates**.

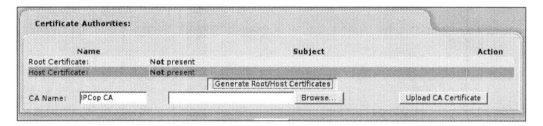

When the next page has loaded, we need to fill out the parameters we wish our X.509 certificate to have. The parameters we need to fill out are **Organisation Name**, **IPCop Hostname**, **E-Mail Address**, **Department**, **City**, **State**, and **Country**.

Generate Root/Host Certificates:

Organization Name:	Some Company
IPCop's Hostname:	172.16.0.128
Your E-mail Address: ●	admin@example.com
Your Department: ●	IT
City: ●	Edinburgh
State or Province: ●	MidLothian
Country:	United Kingdom

[Generate Root/Host Certificates]

● This field may be blank.

WARNING: Generating the root and host certificates may take a long time. It can take up to several minutes on older hardware. Please be patient.

Upload PKCS12 file:	[ ] Browse...
PKCS12 File Password: ●	[ ]

[Upload PKCS12 file]

● This field may be blank.

These should all be relatively self-explanatory — depending upon your environment, you may or may not wish to fill out each field with genuine information. The data entered does not matter, but it will be seen by clients issued with root or host certificates. When this form is filled out, click on the **Generate** button. Since this step involves the generation of certificates, it may (depending upon the specification of your IPCop host) take some time. Feel free to make yourself a coffee at this point.

Once you have completed this step, you should be back at the VPN Configuration page, identical but with the notable exception that the **Root Certificate** and **Host Certificate** entries in the table should be populated, and will have buttons alongside them allowing you to **Download Root Certificate** and **Download Host Certificate**.

Our next step is to download a copy of both host and root certificate files. We do this by clicking on the floppy disk icon at the right-hand side of their entries in the table displayed previously. Both root and host files should be saved to a location on a hard drive or network share, rather than opened or installed on the PC on which you're doing the configuration (unless this is the host you're performing the configuration on).

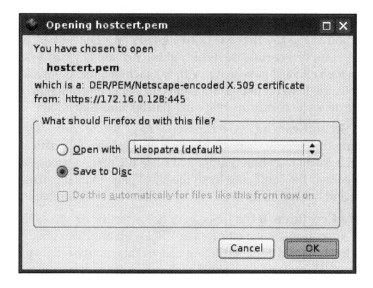

Site-to-Site VPNs Using Certificates

Once we have saved both our host and root certificates using this method, we perform the same process on the other IPCop host. Once this has been done, we import the root and host certificate for each IPCop firewall into the other firewall in the **Authentication** screen when we create our site-to-site VPN, picking the **Upload a Certificate** option rather than the **Use a Pre-Shared Key** option detailed earlier in the chapter.

Once this has been done, both servers will authenticate using certificates rather than PSKs, which adds considerable security to our VPN configuration.

VPN Authentication Options

In the **VPN Authentication** menu, we have four options available to us when configuring the VPN, which impact on how we configure our client:

- **Use a Pre-Shared Key**: As mentioned before, we can only have one VPN configuration using pre-shared keys, and if we are using this configuration we simply need to enter the PSK we have chosen into this field.

- **Upload a Certificate Request**: Generally, when acquiring certificates from a CA (including CAs such as VeriSign and Equifax), it is a common practice to first make a certificate *request* on the system that will have the certificate installed. This is an X.509 certificate with a key generated by the originating system, but which is not signed by any root CA, and so lacks any trust mechanism. By sending this *request* file to a CA (and having the CA process it), we can be sent back a signed copy of the same file. This response file must be re-imported into the machine that made the request (which has the *private* key portion of the key that has been signed), and once it has, is combined to form the complete certificate (with public/private key). In a configuration (such as web cluster) in which multiple machines use the same, signed, certificate, the final certificate should be exported from the originating machine once the certificate response has been re-imported.

Some IPSec software have the capability to generate certificate request files. This being the case, we can simply pick the **Upload a Certificate Request** option in the Authentication dialog, and once IPCop has processed the request file, download the certificate from the VPN page in exactly the same way as the root and host certificates. This certificate can be re-imported into the client

- **Upload a Certificate**: If the IPSec peer has a certificate we wish to use, such as if we are configuring a site-to-site VPN with another IPSec host, we will upload the host and root certificate files in this manner. By uploading our right-hand IPCop host's host and root certificate files into the left-hand IPCop server, and uploading the left-hand IPCop host's host and root certificate files into the right-hand IPCop host, we make both firewalls aware of the other, and can use certificates for a net-to-net VPN.

- **Generate a Certificate**: If the IPSec peer does not handle certificates itself and cannot generate certificate requests, we can generate a certificate from IPCop. This is slightly less secure than using certificate requests, as while using certificate requests at no point is the private key (which is required to use the certificate) transmitted over the open (even if a malicious attacker intercepted the certificate response from the CA, he or she wouldn't be able to do a lot with it), but if we intend to transfer the certificate over a LAN (or enter a strong PKCS12 file password into the generation dialog, which is used to encrypt the certificate), then we can mitigate this risk, to an extent. The resulting certificate from this process can, as with the certificate response method, be downloaded from the VPN page.

Configuring Clients for VPNs

This is a complex topic, and varies vastly on different host platforms. The IPCop Wiki has instructions for Windows clients, which do not have good built-in support for an IPSec VPN.

If we have a VPN configuration using certificates, we will either need to use a client that (like IPCop) has its own CA, or create a certificate using IPCop as detailed earlier. If our VPN requirements are less complex, or we do not want to use certificates, we can use PSKs.

Windows Client Configuration

For client configuration in Windows 2000/XP see: `http://` `www.ipcop.org/modules.php?op=modload&name=ph` `pWiki&file=index&pagename=OpenVPNHowto.`

Linux users have native support from the same packages used by IPCop itself to establish the connection as a server—Linux, BSD, and OSX users should consult their operating system documentation for the most appropriate way to configure this in their environment, as a comprehensive survey of client operating systems is beyond the scope of this book.

The Blue Zone

As of version 1.4, IPCop has had support for a Blue zone, a wireless segment with more aggressive firewall rules than the Orange or Green zones, and designed specifically for an untrusted wireless segment. This could be an open wireless network with access to other networks restricted to some clients, a closed wireless network with an extra layer of security, or even a wired network—it does not have to be wireless.

Wireless security has been the subject of much scrutiny over the last few years. From the lack of understanding of what security measures the 802.11 standards provide to the initially poor security provided by WEP encryption, wireless security is still a sore spot for many IT Departments and manufacturers. Even the improved encryption provided by WPA in Pre-Shared Key and Enterprise (with a radius server) modes is still not enough to satisfy regulatory requirements and corporate policies requiring strong encryption for confidential information.

Better, more secure wireless standards (such as WPA2, the much-anticipated 802.11i) promise to use better versions of today's technology, with improved procedures and stronger encryption—but they are not here at the moment, and many older devices and clients may not support them. For all of these reasons as well as for the peace of mind that defense in depth provides, setting up VPN connections and/or IPSec over wireless networks is very often a good idea.

Traditionally, such setups have been complex and expensive, but IPCop now offers rich, enterprise-grade functionality to even home users.

Prerequisites for a Blue Zone VPN

In order to have a working Blue zone VPN setup, we need an Ethernet card supported by IPCop configured with appropriate IP addressing information (i.e. a non-overlapping private subnet) and with a DHCP server configured to allocate information in the correct address range (i.e. in the same subnet as the IPCop Blue interface and with the Blue interface address as gateway and DNS server).

Setup

The setup for a Blue VPN is identical to a road warrior VPN, with the *Blue* interface configured rather than the *Red* interface.

IPCop Blue VPN Wiki

IPCop has a Wiki page specifically for Blue VPN configuration, which should be updated if and when the setup changes; `http://www.ipcop.org/modules.php?op=modload&name=phpWiki&file=index&pagename=IPCop140BlueVpnHowto`.

Summary

We have covered three common configuration scenarios for the IPCop firewall and IPSec VPNs. Although we have not covered the entire topic end to end, we have hopefully provided enough for you to understand how VPNs work and get your feet wet configuring (hopefully successfully) your IPCop hosts for certificate and Pre-Shared Key-based VPNs. There are many good books written on IPSec, including several volumes on building VPNs with Linux by the publishers of this book (such as `http://www.packtpub.com/openswan/book`, written by the developers of Openswan).

IPSec VPNs, although widely supported, are by no means the easiest to configure. SSL-based VPNs, using the same encryption technology as HTTPS, such as OpenVPN, are quickly becoming popular due to the relative ease of configuration, as well as the simpler nature of the protocol; IPSec, even in conjunction with a protocol such as L2TP, is complex and often broken by firewalls and Network Address Translation.

OpenVPN, in addition to being simpler to firewall, can also run on any number of ports, such as those routinely allowed through firewalls with little or no application-layer inspection, such as 443 or 53. For remote staff finding PPTP or IPSec VPNs difficult and erratic to use, therefore, OpenVPN may be worth looking at. Unfortunately, this ease of use comes at a price—OpenVPN is as yet not widely supported, and although clients exist for Windows and Linux, they aren't in common use, and IPCop does not natively support OpenVPN (although there is an add-on for OpenVPN).

There are resources available on OpenVPN too, including some from this publisher (`http://www.packtpub.com/openvpn/book`) in addition to countless online howtos on OpenVPN generally, and OpenVPN with IPCop (`http://home.arcor.de/ u.altinkaynak/howto_openvpn.html`)

Hopefully, with this material and links to external resources, the curious IPCop administrator is now armed with the information he or she needs to learn more about the subject and possibly pick a subject-specific book to read on the topic!

8
Managing Bandwidth with IPCop

We are now very much aware that IPCop is more than just a basic packet-filtering firewall. We have seen the built-in intrusion detection system as well as the powerful VPN options. Another addition we have is the ability to manage traffic through a couple of different technologies, traffic shaping and caching. We will now look at how we can use these to increase the performance of the network where we need it.

The Bandwidth Problem

In most networks in use at the moment there will generally be a number of different services provided and used by the network and there may be multiple links to other networks. With so many services in place we can use up bandwidth very quickly. The easiest way to ensure you have enough bandwidth for all the services and users on your network is to buy fast links with low contention. This is a good theory, but the economic reality is a little bit more complex, as bandwidth can be expensive and can be a major overhead to a service. In order to combat this, we can work with the services we have and try to reduce their bandwidth usage.

Reducing bandwidth usage can initially be accomplished by using protocols that conserve bandwidth where possible; sometimes, however, we have no choice and have to go with a particular protocol dictated by an application, a vendor, or a user. This is when we can look at reducing the strain put on the network by that application. There are a number of technologies and devices we can use to do this, each with varying complexity and results. IPCop itself, however, has a few simple options to help look after our bandwidth.

The HTTP Problem

One of the most commonly used protocols, Internet-wide, is HTTP (although peer-to-peer filesharing applications are fast catching up). Most businesses have a website running on HTTP as their basic Internet presence and there are very few Internet users that don't use HTTP. We can be pretty confident that this is going to be a protocol used on our network.

HTTP presents us with an important problem when it comes to bandwidth—users expect HTTP to be almost instantaneous. Introducing delays to a user's web browsing experience due to bandwidth congestion is far from an ideal situation and is probably the first place network users are going to notice (and complain!) about a lack of bandwidth. Luckily, IPCop provides us with very powerful options to reduce HTTP's impact on the network.

The Solutions: Proxying and Caching

While use of a proxy isn't a bandwidth-saving measure on its own, it is a feature related to bandwidth control and monitoring. A proxy allows you to monitor, modify, and control requests for web content. You can choose which traffic to log and/or reject as well as modify these requests as they pass through the proxy. Since the proxy sits between the web client and the web server, it can perform some other functions, such as caching.

It's common for users on the same network to access a few of the same websites. This means that every time a user hits the website, they will be downloading all the HTML and images on the page. It would obviously be beneficial for our network if this content was only downloaded once, and then somehow stored to be presented to subsequent clients requesting the same content. Our browsers do that for us at the local level, and so if we access the same page more than once there is a chance our browser has cached a local copy for us.

This is exactly what a caching proxy would provide us, but it would cache for everyone. Whenever a user downloads a page and its images, the proxy will keep a copy in its memory (and/or write it to disk). Whenever a request for the same content appears, rather than passing it to the original website, the proxy provides the client a copy of the cached version of the file. We can reduce bandwidth dramatically, especially if our users are visiting many of the same sites. This does not mean that the information you get will be out of date; a website can request that proxies do not cache information that's time dependent (stock information, weather, and so on).

Introduction to Squid

Squid is one of the most useful and powerful web proxy and caching systems available. It's free and open source, which is why it can be included with IPCop. Squid itself has quite complicated configuration files and performs a variety of proxying and caching functions. As we have come to expect from IPCop, it abstracts this complication nicely and let's us configure Squid with some ease.

Squid was born as a *fork* of Harvest Cached, which was a proxy/caching project and released its first version in 1994, therefore Squid has had a development timeline spanning over 10 years. This has led to a quite stable and full-featured proxying and caching application. The original Harvest Cached project is no longer under development.

Configuring Squid

The Squid configuration screen in IPCop is very easy to follow and you can get away with clicking a couple of boxes for a basic configuration.

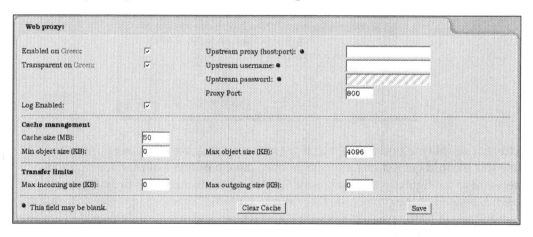

In this example we have only a Green interface present; we can, however, enable the proxy on all other interfaces—except Red, which is the internet connection.

The first step is quite obvious; we enable the proxy on the interfaces we need it on by clicking the first checkbox and then choosing the port the proxy listens on (800 by default in IPCop—although Squid usually runs on port 3128). We can also check the **Log Enabled** box, which is interface non-specific, so we either log all or log none. It's a good idea to enable this if we want to monitor the proxy at some point. We can also chain this proxy through one provided by our ISP for example by configuring the **Upstream** options, which would be provided by the ISP or other proxy service provider. The host port to connect to, and a user name and password may be necessary.

Transparency requires a little more explanation. Traditionally proxies listened on a specific port on the machine, and clients would have to be configured to connect to this. For example, the proxy could be on IP address 10.0.0.1 listening on port 800. In this case we would configure all of our HTTP clients to connect to this proxy. Firefox and Internet Explorer have network settings dialogs where we can configure the proxy access. The Firefox proxy configuration screen is shown in the following figure:

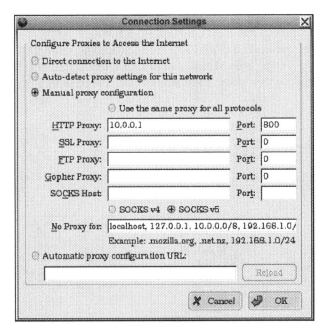

This is a simple method to use, but if we have to configure all of our applications like this it could get tedious, especially if we have a number of machines on the network to configure in the same way. This is where transparent proxying becomes useful. Instead of the proxy listening on one port and forwarding requests through, it monitors all traffic passing through the machine, and where it detects HTTP traffic, it attempts to cache. This also has a downside in that some other protocols may look like HTTP, and an attempt to cache these may break them. If we enable transparent proxying and shortly afterwards an application starts having trouble, it's worth switching the transparency off as an initial step. This is a rare and specific problem but can be quite hard to track down.

Cache Management

Cache size: How much space on disk do we want the cache to take? This is set as a default of 50MB, which is quite sensible for most small networks. If we have a lot of users we may want to increase this to a few 100MB. Going beyond 1 GB on anything but a really large network is rarely necessary. Also, if the number is significantly greater than the available memory on the IPCop machine, then we will have a lot of disk reads/writes, which could slow things down.

Min object size: Sometimes we don't want to cache the really small files as it can be inefficient. Generally, however, it's a good idea to leave this at zero as the repeated HTTP overhead of these files can be a performance hit.

Max object size: Likewise we may not want overly large files to be cached as this will quickly fill up our cache and lead us into the disk read/write problem that we hope to avoid.

The defaults for the previous two options should generally be used unless we have a specific need to change them, for example users continually downloading the same large files.

Transfer Limits

We can also control the maximum and minimum sizes for file transfers through the system. This is not a good idea unless we have a specific case for doing so, as it can be very frustrating for the user. It's quite handy if we want to prevent users downloading very large files such as ISOs, as an attempt to prevent abuse of the network's bandwidth for personal use.

Managing Bandwidth without a Cache

HTTP is not the only protocol on our networks that we need adequate bandwidth for. For example if we have online games or voice and video communication on our network, these services usually warrant higher priority than others due to their time-sensitive use. You wouldn't want to have a choppy voice conversation with a client because one of the users on the network is downloading large files, or on a home network, you wouldn't want to lose your high score in your online game because someone decided to start listening to their online radio station. This is where traffic shaping comes in.

Traffic Shaping Basics

In order to ensure Quality of Service (QoS), we have to control traffic so that high priority traffic is treated as just that, high priority! With traffic shaping, we can use all the same parameters we use in packet filtering; however, instead of deciding whether to pass the traffic, we make more complicated decisions about which traffic is afforded the highest priority and is therefore processed first or given more bandwidth than the other protocols in use on the network.

Traffic is used commonly to control media services. Video- and audio-based services rely heavily on low latency and ample available bandwidth, and so it's common to introduce traffic shaping to a network to accommodate these services.

ISPs Capitalizing on Traffic Shaping

Some ISP's use traffic shaping in much the same way as we describe here, to provide better service to services relying on bandwidth and latency.

There is also another commercial use for this in the form of service provisions. ISPs can traffic shape (and some do) so that one content provider's services respond better than another. For example an ISP can charge for priority shaping, and if Google paid for this service, they would be guaranteed that their content and services would appear faster and more responsive to those of their competitors such as Yahoo! and MSN.

This is an effective way to push out the competition as the ISPs users would likely stick with the *better* content provider. Obviously not entirely in the interests of the ISP's users, but certainly a profitable venture for the ISP and possibly the content providers that pay for these services.

Traffic Shaping Configuration

The traffic shaping configuration page is very simple and could offer us more options, but we have the ability to shape based on port in use, which allows us to be specific enough to differentiate most services for traffic shaping purposes.

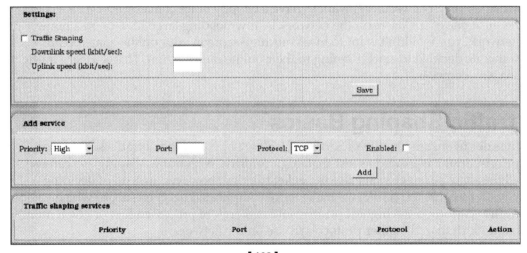

The checkbox next to the words **Traffic Shaping** is used to enable the service. This won't have any effect on the traffic, however, until we define some traffic shaping rules.

We also have to provide the uplink and downlink speeds. This is how fast our network can transfer data out and in. A quick reference to common upload and download speeds is given in the following table, which may not be entirely accurate for our setup. It's recommended we test our own speeds or consult our ISP for more accurate information.

Connection type	Uplink (kbit/sec)	Downlink (kbit/sec)
Dialup	48	56
Cable (1 Meg)	256	1000
T1	192	1540

A more complete guide to different services with their upload and download speeds can be found here: `http://en.wikipedia.org/wiki/List_of_device_bandwidths`.

Adding a Traffic Shaping Service

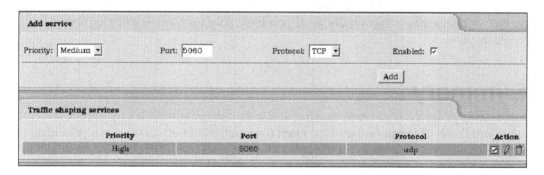

In order to add a service, we fill in the three required fields and then choose **Enabled**. Clicking **Add** adds a new line to the **Traffic shaping services** in the bottom pane. In this case we have added port **5060 UDP** (SIP) as **High** priority, which will ensure that this service is given precedence on the network. These are quite basic traffic shaping options and we don't have the ability to define port ranges or shaping by IP address. We are limited to three levels of priority—low, medium, and high, with ports being added one at a time. It's not necessary to list all ports that will pass through IPCop as those not specified will be handled at medium level by default. To delete this rule, we simply click the trash can on the right-hand side; we can also enable or disable added rules using the checkbox under the **Action** heading.

Editing a Traffic Shaping Service

In order to edit a service we have already added, we can click on the pencil under the action heading, which should show a screen as follows:

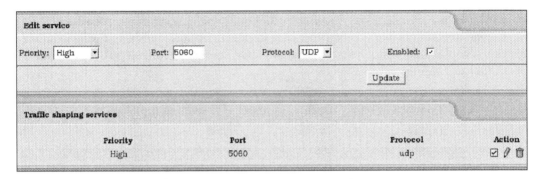

We can see that our rule is now highlighted in yellow in order to make it clear which rule we are editing, and we have the original parameters in the configuration boxes above. The **Add** button has also changed to **Update**. We now modify any value we require and click the **Update** button, which will save the rules and take us back to the initial Traffic Shaping screen.

There are additional modules available for IPCop that extend these capabilities even further, which are worth considering if you have some serious traffic shaping work to accomplish.

Summary

In this chapter we have covered caching and traffic shaping with IPCop and how to configure these. This can be useful on even the smallest of networks, as we prioritize service access, allowing users on the network to be guaranteed the best possible service for any critical services in use. The options for doing so in IPCop are quite basic, and we are limited in the control we have. We have seen, however, that it is possible to make an impact on services in order to improve our bandwidth utilization.

9
Customizing IPCop

IPCop is one of the most full-featured SOHO firewalls on the market and by now you should be familiar with most of the features, but you may have noticed some shortfalls. There may be areas where IPCop doesn't perform a function in exactly the right way or doesn't have a specific function we require. So what can we do? We can customize IPCop with some essential addons.

Addons

At its core IPCop is a collection of Linux-based tools held together with impressive script-based glue. So it's not surprising that we can modify, extend, and improve the system to suit our needs. This is where the community part of open-source software becomes important as we find that users of the system have developed a variety of addons that can be installed and used on IPCop.

Addons are generally developed by third parties, i.e. people other than the IPCop developers. They are usually developed in order to fill some gap that a user found with the software, and then released so that other users can benefit from the work and solve similar problems.

We will take a look at some of the common addons, what they offer, and how we can use them. We can find links to the addons on the IPCop website: `http://ipcop.org/modules.php?op=modload&name=phpWiki&file=index&pagename=IPCopAddons`.

Firewall Addons Server

Firewall addons server allows us a simple, user-friendly and web-based system for managing some addons to IPCop. It is necessary to install this in order to use the addons in this chapter.

We can download the firewall addons server package from
`http://firewalladdons.sourceforge.net/`.

At the time of writing we shall be using the file: `http://heanet.dl.sourceforge.net/sourceforge/firewalladdons/addons-2.3-CLI-b2.tar.gz`

For later versions this location may change and the following commands relating to the filename should be altered to reflect the name of the file downloaded.

First we copy this file to the server using the `scp` command specifying port 222, which is the IPCop default for SSH access, and specify the root user.

```
$ scp -P 222 addons-2.3-CLI-b2.tar.gz  root@10.0.0.200:/
```

We will be prompted for the password for the root account, which is the password we set when installing the IPCop machine.

Now with the file in place we can log in to the IPCop machine and set it up.

```
$ ssh -p 222 root@10.0.0.200
```

P versus p

Notice that a lowercase `-p` is used for the port with `ssh`, and an uppercase `-P` with `scp`. This discrepancy can become quite annoying and can lead to hard-to-spot typos. If you can't get a connection, check if you are using the correct case for the command.

After entering the root password we should see the following prompt:

```
root@ipcop:~ #
```

We now type the following commands to set up the addons server:

```
# mv /addons /addons.bak
# tar xzvf /addons-2.3-CLI-b2.tar.gz -C /
# cd /addons
# ./addoncfg -u
# ./addoncfg -i
```

After the commands complete, we log in to the IPCop web interface and should see an addition to the menu along the top of the page.

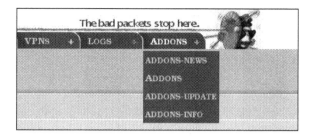

We will take a look at the few new pages our web interface now has, and the added options they offer.

The **ADDONS-NEWS** page shows updates about the firewall addons server and the addons it provides. There are no configuration options here other than how much news we would like to see. It serves as a general information page using important news downloaded from the addons website.

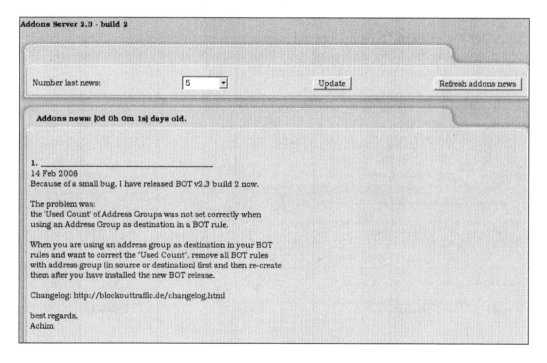

The **ADDONS** page gives information about the addons installed and current addons available, and allows us to install or remove addons.

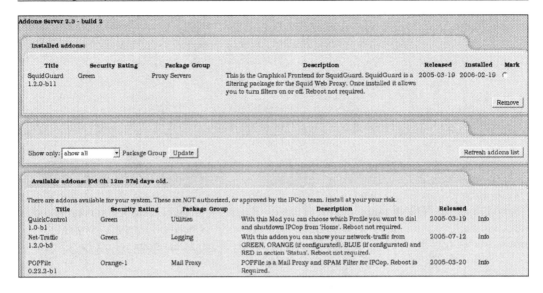

The **ADDONS-UPDATE** page gives us information on updates for addons in much the same way as the **ADDONS** page did about the addons themselves, showing what is available, and providing us with a method for installing updates.

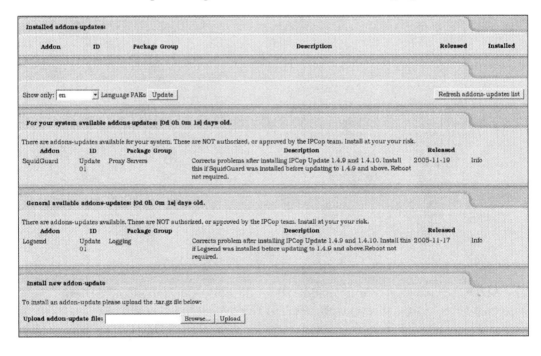

Installing Addons

Now that we are familiar with the interface of the firewall addons server, we can start installing and using addons. We will begin with SquidGuard, which as you might have noticed was installed in the previous screenshots. To install an addon we go to the **ADDONS** page and scroll down until we see the addon we would like to install. We then click on the **Info** hyperlink on the right-hand side, which takes us to a detailed information and download page for the addon. In the case of SquidGuard this page is `http://firewalladdons.sourceforge.net/squidguard.html`.

On this page we get detailed information on the plug-in and are provided with download links to the current version; at the time of writing this was: `http://heanet.dl.sourceforge.net/sourceforge/firewalladdons/SquidGuard-1.2.0-GUI-b11.tar.gz`. This may well be updated, and so check the earlier link first!

We download the addon, which comes in a GZIPPED TAR archive. We then go back to the **ADDONS** page, click the **Browse** button, browse to the file we just downloaded, click **Upload**, and the addon is installed on the server.

Caution: Sometimes when uploading an addon, especially those such as SquidGuard that restart the web server, we don't have the page being refreshed automatically and/or the connection might time out. Hitting **Refresh**, or **Stop** then **Refresh** in the browser should bring us back to the **ADDONS** page.

The process is similar for all other addons that are installed with the firewall addons server, and so there is no need for us to repeat the steps later on, when we look at other addons and how they work.

Common Addons

We will now have a look at the configuration of some of the more common addons and how they are used. Since we have SquidGuard installed already, we can begin with this addon. We won't cover all of the addons in this text as they are quite numerous. We will, however, cover the most common and substantial ones. It's recommended that we at least familiarize ourselves with the other addons available, as they may fill a requirement we might later come to recognize.

SquidGuard

SquidGuard is a content-filtering plug-in, which can be installed with Squid. It is used primarily to block unsuitable content from the Web and can be configured with a dynamic set of rules, which include blanket bans of various subjects and/or black-and white-listing of sites depending on their perceived suitability for the audience on our network.

The SquidGuard configuration screen looks like this:

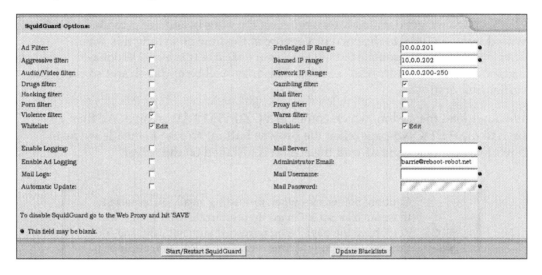

As we can see, we can filter on a variety of subjects, which are pre-defined in the SquidGuard configuration.

In the screenshot above, we have chosen to filter advertisements, porn, violence, and gambling related sites from our network.

We have also configured a few other options to aid in controlling our network usage. We have determined that the machine at IP address **10.0.0.201** is a privileged machine (possibly our own or an administrator's machine), which is allowed to bypass the filters and access sites indiscriminately. **10.0.0.202** is in the **Banned IP range** and is a machine that isn't allowed to access any resources on the Internet through this web proxy. The **Network IP Range** denotes all other users on the network that will be subjected to the other rules configured earlier. Notice that the **Network IP Range** includes machines **200-250**; all the other ranges can be specified similarly allowing us to include more than one IP address in the rule if necessary.

We also have some other important and powerful configuration options here. If we allow white-listing and then click on the **Edit** box, we see the following screen:

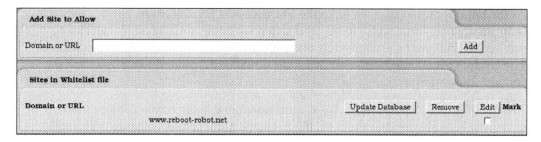

By entering a URL and clicking **Add** we allow access to this domain regardless of any other rules in place. In this case the URL www.reboot-robot.net has been white-listed.

The blacklist configuration screen is exactly the same and any domains listed there are blocked by SquidGuard except the privileged IP addresses.

Other than the direct configuration of what to block and not to block, we have some other options that require some explanation.

- **Enable Logging**: Allows us to log connections allowed and denied by SquidGuard
- **Enable Ad Logging**: Allows more detailed logging of the advertisements blocked
- **Mail Logs**: Log information on mail passing through the firewall
- **Automatic Update**: Download automatic updates of URLs for blocking from the SquidGuard website
- **Mail Server**: Server to be used when sending mail to the administrator
- **Administrator Email**: The email address to send logs to
- **Mail username**: Username to be used if mail server requires authentication
- **Mail Password**: Password to be used as earlier

Mail Settings

You will notice these mail settings as part of any addon that offers communication with a network administrator. It's worth keeping this information handy and possibly creating an email account/address specifically for our IPCop machine.

The only boxes that are required on this page are our **Network IP Range** and our **Administrator Email**; everything else can be configured optionally (optional fields have a blue star beside them).

At the bottom of the page we have the **Start/Restart SquidGuard** button, which is (admittedly non-intuitively) to be used when we have configured the service to our needs, and want the configuration saved and used on the running machine. The **Update Blacklists** button allows us to download updated blacklists for the content-filtering options.

After configuring SquidGuard, we should now have an effective content filtering system to help ensure that users on the network don't access websites considered undesirable.

What if we want to monitor as well as control? The attentive reader might have realized while we enabled the logging options that there should be access to these logs, possibly in the web interface. If we move the mouse above **Logs**, sure enough we see **SquidGuard Logs**; clicking on this will give us:

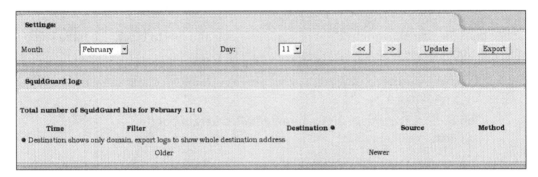

This allows us to view the SquidGuard logs in an interface similar to the default logs on the system.

Enhanced Filtering

The Enhanced Filtering addon is one of the most useful addons and addresses what is one feature that IPCop is sorely lacking by default. A default installation of IPCop will allow all traffic outbound from the Green interface to the other interfaces without any filtering. It's often desirable to control the ports and IP addresses that a user can access from the Green interface. For example, we may want to block all outbound connections except those to the ports websites run on. This would allow for default blocking of peer-to-peer filesharing programs and instant messaging programs. This is the preferred default setup for a firewall, which we discussed in Chapter 3. Enhanced Filtering also allows for MAC-based filtering of the wireless connection.

Port and IP-Based Blocks Aren't Completely Effective

Be aware that blocking the port an application is using doesn't prevent users using that application on another port or through a proxy server located outside the IPCop protected network. Similarly IP-based blocks can be overcome by using proxies. Application-layer filtering adds to this protection, but without stringent control of the internal resources on the network, most network-level filtering mechanisms can be bypassed.

For more information refer to the Enhanced Filtering web page:
`http://firewalladdons.sourceforge.net/filtering.html`.

The version used at the time of writing was downloaded from the following URL and is installed in a manner similar to SquidGuard:

`http://heanet.dl.sourceforge.net/sourceforge/firewalladdons/`
`EnhancedFiltering-1.0-GUI-b2.tar.gz`

The following figure shows the Enhanced Filtering configuration screen, which can be accessed by clicking on **Firewall | Enhanced Filtering**:

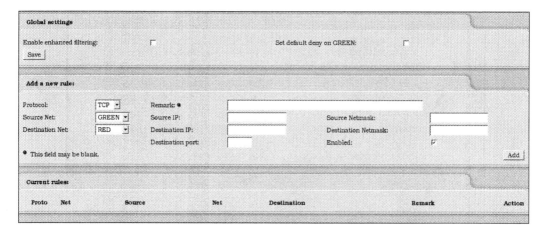

Here we can **Enable enhanced filtering** or **Disable** it as well as **Set default deny on GREEN** network interface. We discussed default deny when we introduced firewalls, and why it's an easier-to-manage and more secure setup.

We can also add specific rules to the firewall for connections between networks. We have to provide the source and destination IP addresses, source netmask and destination netmask, network, and the destination port.

An example would be allowing only our mailserver to connect outwards to our ISP's mailserver in order to relay mail for the network. We would specify the **Source IP** address as that of our mail server and the **Destination IP** address as that of the ISP's mailserver, also setting the port to **25**. This means that our mail server can relay mail to the ISP but no other machines on the network can. This would help prevent our users using outside mail accounts, and prevent machines with malware sending copies of the malware or spam out, without passing through our mail server and potentially mail filtering software.

The main advantage as we can now see is that we can control very specifically which servers and services on those servers our local network machines can access, which is functionality that IPCop itself doesn't provide by default.

Blue Access

Another option provided by the Enhanced Filtering addon is the ability to filter the Blue (wireless) interface based on IP address and MAC address. This is a crude but fairly effective way of limiting access to the wireless interface to machines with a specific MAC address. A MAC address is unique to a Network Interface Card and is a fairly useful method for identifying a card. MAC address filtering is by no means an alternative to encrypting the wireless connection, but is a useful secondary measure.

MAC Spoofing

MAC addresses are easily spoofed with tools existing for most common OSs to modify the MAC address of a NIC. The MAC address isn't modified in the device itself, but in the operating system. Linux, for example, can do this with its default network configuration tool ifconfig, and many tools exist for Windows to accomplish the same task. There is an addon for IPCop that provides MAC spoofing functionality in the GUI for the Red interface.

The **Blue Access** configuration screen can be accessed by clicking
Firewall | Blue Access:

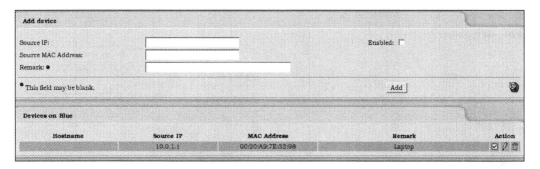

The **Source IP** and **Source MAC Address** are filled with the information of the
machine being allowed to access the network from this interface, and when the
Enabled checkbox is ticked, only the machines that match the list will be allowed
to access any network resources. The machines in the **Devices on Blue** list are those
that have been allowed access.

LogSend

LogSend is an addon that allows us to send logs from the IPCop machine to various
administrators and/or to the DShield service. This is useful as it allows deeper
analysis of our logs using external tools, without configuring a syslog server.

The LogSend web page is found at:
`http://firewalladdons.sourceforge.net/logsend.html`.

The current version used at time of writing is: `http://heanet.dl.sourceforge.`
`net/sourceforge/firewalladdons/Logsend-1.0-GUI-b3.tar.gz`.

The **LogSend Configuration** page is accessed by clicking **Logs | LogSend**.

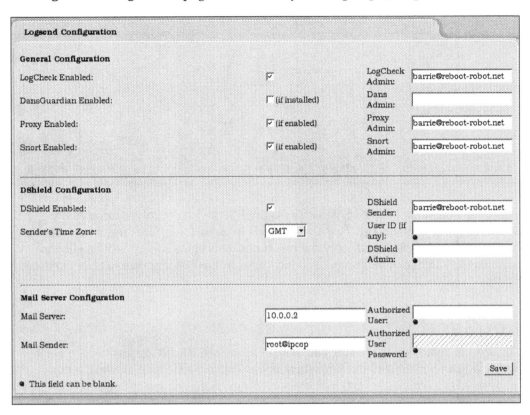

The configuration for **LogCheck** is relatively simple; we can choose to enable the service, enable mailing of **DansGuardian** (provided by the Cop+ addon) logs, **Proxy** logs, and **Snort** logs. Each of these could go to a different administrator but it's very common for the same email address to be used in each as shown in the figure above.

DShield

The **DShield** option may need some explanation. DShield (http://www.dshield.org) is a service proved by SANS (System Administration, Networking, and Security Institute: http://www.sans.org). It collates and analyses logs from thousands of systems around the world in order to get details on the most commonly attacked ports and the worst offending attacking IP addresses. This is in an effort to allow system administrators to be aware of the current state of the Internet at any point in time. Any logs sent to DShield will be added to this database, and if we sign up for a DShield account (not required for sending logs), we can also use its online analyzing tools to monitor the data from our own Intrusion Protection Systems.

The DShield configuration function in LogSend enables easy use of the DShield service so that we can send our logs. All that is required is we enable DShield, and set a time zone and a return email address to use when sending the logs. If we also provide our user ID, we can ensure that the logs are attributed to our account and available to us on the DShield web interface. The **DShield Administrator** is the address to which any log information will be sent.

We also have the familiar mailserver options where we can provide the mailserver to use, the sender, and any authentication credentials required. We have seen these options in other areas of IPCop.

Copfilter

Copfilter extends IPCop from a firewall into a security appliance similar to those provided by Symantec and MacAfee, which attempt to protect our network from all manner of malware. Copfilter will monitor web, FTP, and email traffic in order to detect and block malware it finds within the data.

The Copfilter web page is: http://www.copfilter.org.

The version used at time of writing was: http://heanet.dl.sourceforge.net/sourceforge/copfilter/copfilter-0.82.tgz.

Copfilter installation is done directly and not via the addons interface. It is installed in much the same way that the firewall addons server was installed.

```
$ scp -P 222 copfilter-0.82.tgz root@10.0.0.200:/ # provide password
$ ssh -p 222 root@10.0.0.200 # provide password
```

```
# cd /
# tar xzvf copfilter-0.82.tgz
# cd copfilter-0.82
# ./install
```

We should then see the following output:

```
===============================================================
Copfilter installation --  Version 0.82
===============================================================
WARNING:
This package is NOT an official ipcop addon. It has not been approved
or reviewed by the ipcop development team. It comes with NO warranty or
guarantee, so use it at your own risk.
This package adds firewall rules, proxies, filters, virus scanners
and precompiled binaries to your ipcop machine,
Do NOT use Copfilter if firewall security is an issue
Continue ? [y/N]
```

It gives us a warning that installing Copfilter reconfigures the firewall and may alter some of its functionality, possibly reducing security.

Complexity and Security

This brings in an important point we should consider when installing addons. The more code and features we add to a firewall, the more scope there is for something to go wrong. Software bugs lead to crashes and more importantly security compromises. It's important to weigh the value given by a feature against the potential risk of having additional code in the system before we fill the system up with a variety of addons.

Copfilter should now install, and we will see a few messages scroll by as it sets itself up. We should see the following message when Copfilter is completely installed:

```
Copfilter 0.82 installation completed successfully !
```

If we now log into the web interface, we should see new menu options added to the IPCop configuration site. We will have a look at them in the next few sections.

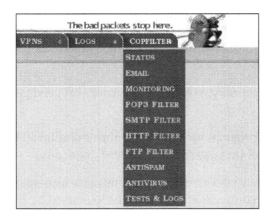

Status

The **Status** screen gives us information on the tools installed with Copfilter (yet another collection of powerful tools in a simple package!). You can start and stop all services here. By clicking on the **Virus Quarantine** and **Spam Quarantine** buttons, you can see the items that have been held there by the scanning software.

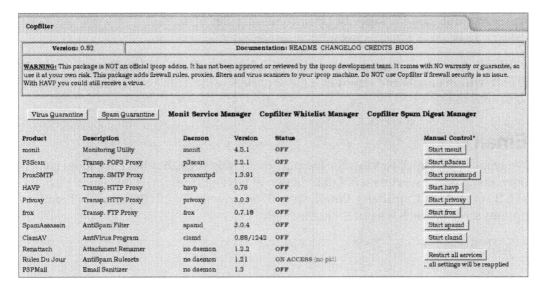

monit: Allows us to monitor the system in more detail than the basic status information provided by IPCop, with management of services as an important addition (`http://www.tildeslash.com/monit/`).

p3Scan: Proxy server for email (**POP3**) to scan email for malware (`http://p3scan.sourceforge.net/`).

ProxySMTP: Similar to **p3scan** but used for scanning SMTP.

HAVP: Proxy for HTTP, which allows scanning of websites for malware (http://www.server-side.de/).

Privoxy: Another HTTP proxy, which focuses more on privacy and advertisements (http://www.privoxy.org).

frox: Transparent FTP proxy, which allows features similar to **HAVP** and **Privoxy** against the FTP protocol (http://frox.sourceforge.net).

Spamassassin: Extremely powerful and customizable anti-spam software. This is one of the most common anti-spam solutions used by ISPs (http://spamassassin.apache.org/).

ClamAV: Antivirus software, used in conjunction with some of the other software to provide a virus scanning engine (http://www.clamav.net/).

Renattach: Script that recognizes and renames dangerous email attachments such as .exe, .bat, and .pif so as to prevent users accidentally or unintentionally opening dangerous files (http://freshmeat.net/projects/renattach/).

Rules Du Jour: Used to keep the SpamAssassin rules up to date (http://www.exit0.us/index.php?pagename=RulesDuJour).

P3PMail: Acts like p3Scan mentioned earlier; however it detects dangerous HTML within emails and removes it (http://www.exit0.us/index.php?pagename=RulesDuJour).

Email

We want to enable all services for the purpose of this book, but if we try to do so now, many of the services will fail because we haven't configured our email settings yet. If we click on **Copfilter | Email**, we will be presented with the familiar **Email** options screen, which we can fill accordingly.

Email:			
Email address :	ipcop@reboot-robot.net	SMTP-AUTH enabled:	off
SMTP server:	10.0.0.2	SMTP-AUTH user: ●	
Sender address: ●	ipcop@reboot-robot.net	SMTP-AUTH password: ●	

No service restart required
Save settings

● This field may be blank.

With this filled in, we can start enabling and configuring services.

Monitoring

monit is very easy to set up (in Copfilter) and quite a powerful and dependable tool. As the **Monitoring** screen (click **Copfilter | Monitoring**) shows, **monit** will constantly monitor running services and will restart any failed services within 60 seconds. Stopping a service manually will cause monitoring for that service to be switched off. To switch monitoring back on for all services, a restart of **monit** itself is required.

We can switch on **monit** in this configuration window. We should switch it on just now so that it is available to monitor the other services, so select **On** in the drop-down box and click the **Save** button.

POP3 Filtering

POP3 is a commonly used mail protocol, for receiving mail. If we have users pulling email down from an ISP's mail server, then we can configure this screen to filter any mail coming in via POP3 and tune it to our needs.

We should be careful with quarantining email or attachments as this can very quickly start to fill space on our hard drive. If we have provisioned a low specification machine to use as the IPCop box, then we may have trouble with hard drive space. If this begins to cause problems, simply back up the IPCop configuration and reinstall on a bigger hard drive.

Configure this screen as shown in the previous figure and then push the **Save settings (and restart services)** button. This will enable POP3 scanning. Notifications will be sent to the email address we configured in the email screen earlier.

SMTP Filtering

This page at first glance appears the same as the POP3 page but with an SMTP slant (and it should be configured identically for our use here). However, as we scroll down we see:

Enable ProxSMTP to filter incoming traffic on RED and forward to internal Email Server * ***	on ▾	Discard (delete) all SMTP virus emails (virus quaranting and virus notifications will be disabled)	off ▾
Email Server is located in network	ORANGE ▾	Discard (delete) all SMTP spam emails if ...	off ▾
Email Server IP Address	10.0.0.2	... if score is greater than: (spam quaranting above this score will be disabled)	20 ▾
Red IP Alias Address (if this is empty the current RED IP Address will be used)		Discard (delete) all SMTP emails with dangerous attachments	off ▾
Red IP Alias Ethernet Interface	eth1:1 ▾		
Add email addresses from outgoing email to Copfilter**** Whitelist	on ▾	Enable Copfilter Whitelist modifications via email*****	off ▾
Disable all spam scanning on outgoing email from internal network	off ▾	Use Copfilter Whitelist and Blacklist +++	on ▾
Quarantine spam emails if ...	on ▾	Quarantine virus infected emails	off ▾
... if score is greater than:	15 ▾		
Send user a copy of quarantined spam email	off ▾	Remove emails in quarantine if older than (in days)	14

This gives us some additional options mostly relating to the email server on our network. We discussed previously the use of a DMZ and IPCop using the Orange network for the DMZ. If we had our email server in a DMZ, we could configure port 25 (or port 25 on a specific IP) to be forwarded to our email server. Since this is the SMTP filtering section and not the port forwarding section, we could also filter all email as it goes through the system before it gets near our server. This allows us to protect machines in our DMZ from attack and subsequently protects our users as the malware-ridden emails won't ever touch their inbox!

The configuration options shown are fairly reasonable levels, unless we require whitelisting or have specific quarantining requirements.

HTTP Filter (and FTP)

The HTTP filter is among the most resource-intensive features of Copfilter, mainly because HTTP traffic involves large files and quite detailed scanning, and because HTTP is one of the most popular protocols in use on most networks.

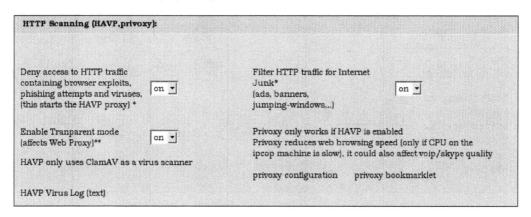

It's generally a good idea to configure the HTTP proxy as transparent as this won't require reconfiguration of the client machines. As noted on this screen, this can adversely affect applications passing through the firewall, if the firewall becomes very busy. It may not be a good idea to use HTTP filtering on a busy network unless the IPCop machine is quite powerful. If you are experiencing slowness when using the Internet, disable HTTP filtering as one of the initial troubleshooting steps.

The FTP filter is very simple to set up and requires merely a switch from off to on. It works in much the same way as the transparent HTTP filter. FTP filter is less commonly used as it is a much less popular protocol than HTTP and there are many other file transfer methods more popular than FTP now.

AntiSPAM

In addition to fighting malware, we also have a constant battle against the deluge of spam landing in our mailbox daily. Luckily the Copfilter options for spam are relatively simple.

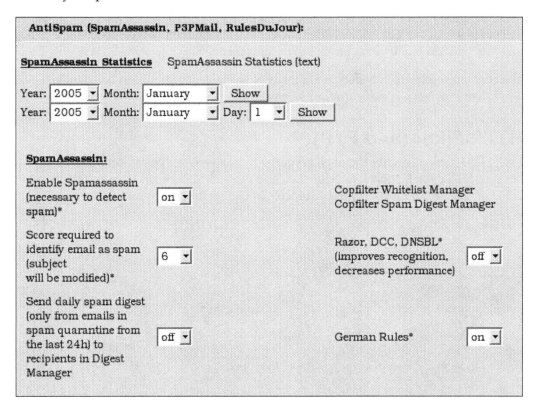

Once enabled, we can configure the score at which to consider an email as spam. Each message is checked for various spam-like traits; the more traits it has, the higher the score it gets. If we set this threshold too high, then we will allow some spam through, and if we set it too low, we increase the chances of false positives. The default works remarkably well and should be used unless a large volume of spam is getting through. We can also configure Bayesian filtering on this page. However this can be very resource intensive and it's not recommended on a box that is also providing many other functions. Turning **on** German rules will prevent German language spam coming through the filter; this is provided due to a large increase of spam being sent out in German. The option for **Razor, DCC, DNSBL** enables blocking based on databases of known spamming sites, these can be fairly large and as noted on the configuration screen they may decrease performance.

AntiVirus

ClamAV is very commonly used on Linux systems as a virus scanner. However, it covers viruses from a variety of operating systems and obviously its largest signature database relates to the Windows platform. So it is excellent for protecting Windows clients on the network from virus attacks. ClamAV is used as the scanning engine for the other tools in Copfilter, and so is already enabled by the time we get to it because the other services are using it.

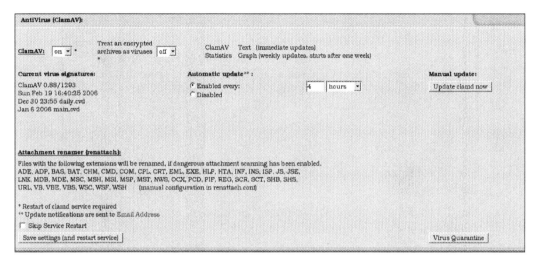

We may want to tweak when the automatic updates are applied as well as perform manual updates of ClamAV, especially shortly after installation. We can also add other file extensions to the `renattach` configuration file from this menu such as WMF. These files will be renamed so as to have an extension that won't execute automatically with a double-click.

WMF and Media File Vulnerabilities

Recently there was a very serious and highly publicized vulnerability in Microsoft Windows, which could be exploited if the user viewed an image in WMF format. This highlighted the often-ignored fact that not just executable files can contain executable code.

Tests and Logs

The Copfilter addon has its own area for logs, sadly choosing to shy away from adding options to the **Logs** menu as other addons do. In this area we can view and download a variety of logs in various formats; however, they are too numerous to warrant coverage in this text. The logs are relatively easy to read and understand, and the documentation on the websites of the projects mentioned earlier will give more information on these.

Three other important functions here are the test buttons.

- **Send Test Virus Email**: This button sends an email with the EICAR test virus.

> **EICAR**
>
> EICAR is a test virus definition that all antivirus software recognizes. It's used as a calibration tool to ensure that our anti-virus solution is working without having to send a virus through our network.
>
> http://www.eicar.org/anti_virus_test_file.htm

- **Send Test Spam Email**: Sends an email that should be picked up as Spam by the Spam filters.
- **Send Test Email +dang. Attachment**: Sends a dangerous attachment through email to test the functionality of renattach.

It's important to run each of these tests and maybe a few manual runs at sending tests through the filters before trusting the setup with the protection of our network resources.

Up and Running!

If we now have a look at the status screen, we should see that all of the services have been started and are being monitored and controlled.

Product	Description	Daemon	Version	Status	Manual Control*
monit	Monitoring Utility	monit	4.5.1	ON (PID 3933 3932 3931)	Stop monit
P3Scan	Transp. POP3 Proxy	p3scan	2.2.1	ON (PID 1200)	Stop p3scan
ProxSMTP	Transp. SMTP Proxy	proxsmtpd	1.3.91	ON (PID 3850)	Stop proxsmtpd
HAVP	Transp. HTTP Proxy	havp	0.76	ON (PID 1961 1960 ...)	Stop havp
Privoxy	Transp. HTTP Proxy	privoxy	3.0.3	ON (PID 2010)	Stop privoxy
frox	Transp. FTP Proxy	frox	0.7.18	ON (PID 2469)	Stop frox
SpamAssassin	AntiSpam Filter	spamd	3.0.4	ON (PID 2946 2945 2911)	Stop spamd
ClamAV	AntiVirus Program	clamd	0.88/1293	ON (PID 983 520)	Stop clamd
Renattach	Attachment Renamer	no daemon	1.2.2	ON ACCESS (no pid)	Restart all services
Rules Du Jour	AntiSpam Rulesets	no daemon	1.21	ON ACCESS (no pid)	.. all settings will be reapplied
P3PMail	Email Sanitizer	no daemon	1.3	ON ACCESS (no pid)	

Summary

We have seen that IPCop can be more than just a simple NAT firewall. It can handle multiple network zones and treat each of these independently. We can have real control over how these network segments can communicate with each other. A firewall can do much more than just filter — it can control, monitor, and report on the network's status giving us a good overall view of how our network is functioning, and IPCop can fulfill these requirements.

We have also seen IPCop as a network appliance similar to the expensive commercial offerings from many vendors. In this respect IPCop can handle advanced firewalling with some application-level or layer-seven filtering. We discussed this earlier and IPCop's layer-seven shortcomings. We now see how we can address this and any other problems to create a truly useful and powerful perimeter device.

We looked at the various addons available for IPCop and had a fairly detailed look at some of the most commonly used ones and the useful options available. We have seen some of the direct benefits of using open source software such as IPCop in its simple extensibility or "*hackability*". We covered some advanced proxying options with SquidGuard and its use on IPCop. We also looked at Copfilter — one of the most popular IPCop addons — with it's filtering of many common protocols for malware and other undesirable traffic. We've only scratched the surface of IPCop addons, however, as there are many more out there. Everything from an installation of Nmap on IPCop to a SETI client! It's worth exploring the options available, as those presented here serve only to give an overview of the common applications.

10
Testing, Auditing, and Hardening IPCop

In this chapter, we will examine some common attitudes towards security and patch management, and discuss how we may want to treat these topics within the context of IPCop. We will also discuss some common security risks, some common security and auditing tools and tests, and find out where to go next.

Security and Patch Management

Security is, very loosely, the process of keeping our systems in such a state that either they are deemed to be impractical to break into, or in which the vulnerabilities and risks entailed in keeping those systems operational are understood, managed, and either compensated for or accepted. Contrary to received wisdom (and intuition, for some), there is no such thing as a secure system.

There is a well-used aphorism among the security community, *"Security is a journey, not a destination."*

The best security consultant, programmer, or IT professional in the world is only able to secure a computer system to the extent that the hardware and software he or she is working with allows. Even a perfectly set up, textbook deployment of a secure software package runs the risk that an application component, operating system component, or piece of hardware may have a fault or develop a fault compromising the security of the system. A software fault may do any number of things—it may allow an intruder to gain information, cause a system to function improperly, or even gain control of that system.

A relatively harmless fault providing the attacker solely with information may provide him or her with the information needed to further research other flaws in the software running on that computer system—leading to further compromise, possibly leading to gaining control of the system.

Further more, whatever any vendor, professional, or developer tells you, there is *no* solution, be it a shiny new piece of software, a shiny new piece of hardware, a decrepit old security guru, or a clever configuration change that will solve all of your security problems. They (can) all add up, but *there is no such thing as a panacea.*

All that we can hope to do is bear these principles in mind in layering our environment such that we do not rely on any one security measure wherever possible, and such that damage is limited. Indeed, firewalls similar to IPCop are used in larger organizations to segregate different networks and subnets for precisely this reason.

The process of keeping our systems as secure as possible has two important components that we are concerned with here.

The first, and most basic, is that of keeping the software running on our systems up-to-date. A comprehensive firewall strategy, excellent set of permissions, and strong set of passwords count for virtually nothing, if the software we are running is out of date and therefore has holes in it. While there are probably security flaws in most of the software packages we use that have not yet been discovered, if we (and the developers of the software) don't know that they're there, the chances that an intruder does are reduced as well. If the flaw is known to the developers (and worse yet, if it is patched), we should automatically assume that any attacker wanting to break into our system knows about it too. An unpatched system is significantly harder to secure than a patched system.

The second, and more difficult step, is the process of **system hardening**. This may involve any number of steps from changing filing system permissions and putting in place a firewall policy, to surrounding our systems with intrusion prevention systems, physical security measures (such as locks and CCTV), and even taking regular backups (being able to go back in time and check what our system looked like is often critically important to analysis of a system we believe may be compromised).

Why We Should Be Concerned

For some readers, this topic may seem fairly obvious while for others, used to thinking about IT and about computers in general from a different standpoint, it may not. It has been the experience of the authors that quite frequently extremely competent managers, IT professionals, and computer scientists are quite unaware of how computers can be abused, how much damage this abuse can do, and how easy these things are to accomplish.

However, disregarding this misunderstanding for a moment, there are many well-meaning managers, home users, and IT professionals who do understand that computers can be broken into, and are aware that there is more that they can do to secure their system. This gives birth to one of the greatest myths in wide circulation, a viewpoint that is often held very strongly by people with large clout within organizations of every size. This is a *wrong* viewpoint for any organization valuing its ability to make money and using computers to do so (that nowadays is practically everyone), or any home user using his or her PC for such things as accounting, online banking, or online shopping. This fallacy, of *"why would anyone want to do that to us?"* is based on the premise that the sole threat to computers is determined attackers specifically picking companies based on their identity and as a home user, small business, or dull manufacturing company, one is immune.

Of course, viruses, worms, adware, and spyware—four of the most common issues being dealt with by security and IT professionals—have nothing to do with companies being targeted, and some of the biggest (and most costly) incidents to deal with result in loss of image or legal liability as a result of actions carried out by intruders, using a company's system as a springboard to break into others. Such problems can be devastating for home users whose credit card is stolen, who suffer from identity theft, or are legally liable as a result of someone abusing their online auction account.

A quick survey of the many, many papers on disaster recovery on the Web brings up different versions of the same statistic again and again—that *X% of companies experiencing Y days of downtime never recover from [a disaster].* X and Y vary from paper to paper, but invariably X is a double-figure number, and Y is a single figure. This alone should be reason to keep your systems secure from an intruder who could wipe out your data and destroy your ability to do business—whether business constitutes running an actual company or simply being able to file your home taxes.

All this assumes that we have no regulatory requirements—exploring standards such as ISO 17799 is well outside our scope, and many regulations and standards (including ISO 17799) include stipulations regarding business continuity and disaster recovery planning.

The fact that you have this book and that you're reading this section of this chapter probably means that this text is preaching to the converted, but at least—hopefully—you may be armed with some useful points if you ever encounter anyone who hasn't been converted yet!

Appliances and How this Affects Our Management of IPCop

Now that we have explored the notions of security and disaster recovery briefly, we can move on to how this actually affects our ongoing management and securing of IPCop. To venture into another common failing within IT, firewalls (alongside networked devices such as printers, switches, and routers) are some of the least cared for devices out there. A large majority of small and medium businesses simply do not perform any routine management on these devices, frequently leaving switches and routers that may be exposed to the Internet with software versions running on them that may be full of holes for an intruder to exploit! Services such as **Simple Network Management Protocol** (**SNMP**), which are shipped on many devices with the default community strings (acting similarly to passwords) of public/private, frequently allow intruders to take complete control of a device (sometimes more powerfully than via the device's web configuration interface) simply and quietly.

Another common preconception fueling this neglect is the assumption that because a device isn't a PC and doesn't have a screen, keyboard, or mouse, it isn't a computer and doesn't require updating. The broad userbase of the Internet, and the number of products designed to operate as routers, firewalls, etc., has not helped this.

The Appliance, a computer that is not a computer, has a strong influence on this. *Appliances*, broadly, are computers designed to operate without the management and updates that *normal*, software-centric servers require. Unfortunately, many of these appliances are based on software similar to that for non-appliance devices, and although appliances are typically more tightly locked down and secured than an equivalent server set up to do the same job, they are not exempt from similar security issues.

Our IPCop system is designed to operate similarly to an appliance. It is entirely designed and updated by one set of individuals (the IPCop team), it is running on a PC, and it is based on a normal operating system tailored in order to provide a very specific function (and exposing little of the operation of the operating system) — so to some extent we need to treat it as one. We should (as with any appliance) still update our system via the firmware, and must still avoid prying too much into the workings of the firewall if we wish it to remain operational (and supportable), but an understanding of what goes on under the covers and how it works is very beneficial to our securing of IPCop.

Basic Firewall Hardening

First and foremost, we need to consider how IPCop looks to the outside world. The first step taken by any hacker, penetration tester, IT professional, or analyst in assessing the threat that a particular device poses, whether they intend to fix it or break in via it, is to profile that device in order to find out some of the following things:

- What the device is
- What operating system it is running
- What sort of hardware it may be running on
- What services the server is running, and therefore by inference...
- What software (services) the server is running in addition to the basic operating system
- Whether any of the above (particularly the services) are insecure

As a legitimate auditor, manager, and maintainer of IPCop systems, much of this is available to us from memory, from our documentation, or by logging into the host itself. For an attacker, to whom such information is extremely valuable, this is not the case, and so it behooves us to understand how an intruder would gather such information, in order to prevent him or her from doing so.

Checking What Exposure Our Firewall Has to Clients

The most basic tool in assessing what our IPCop box looks like from the outside is the port scanner. As we should be aware from earlier in the book, a server may open any number of ports in order to allow users to connect to services it runs. We should also know that IPCop may have at least one port open to internal clients by default—port 445, which is the port HTTPS runs over for configuration via the web interface. A port scanner, very simply, attempts to connect to lots of different ports, and sees which ports it gets replies from, defining these as open (i.e. there's something going on at the other end).

Port scanning is an important exercise to carry out on infrastructure like firewalls as part of a security audit or periodic checkup for several reasons. The most notable of these is that we may not always know what our servers are running. We can get a list of which ports our firewall thinks it has open either by using the `netstat` command at a shell, or viewing them via the web interface. If, however, we are scanning our server because we believe that a malicious intruder may have installed software on our firewall for nefarious purposes, the fact that that software has an open port (for instance, to allow the intruder to re-connect and gain access through a backdoor) may be hidden from the `netstat` command and certain portions of the operating system itself.

Scanning the system independently in this situation is one of the few ways to detect such activity, and for this reason if you're serious about security, it is good to get into the habit of doing it periodically; you can't be too prudent.

Port Scanning via the Internet

Many Internet Service Providers have quite strict policies with regard to port scanning via their networks, and will treat any such activity as illegitimate, even though there is nothing illegal about port scanning your own server (and the port scanning of systems that are not your own is considered by many to be a legal grey area, although increasingly being treated as criminal activity in itself). Many more reasonable ISPs will make the distinction between port scanning your own systems, which you (obviously) have consent to do, and the port scanning of others. Some, though, are a little more judgmental (some would employ the use of the word illiberal!).

Intensively scanning all traffic for this sort of activity traversing an ISP's network is very resource intensive, and ISPs will rarely do this to traffic that is not destined for their servers (or high-value systems in general) due to the expense required. It is, however, worth checking your ISP's terms and conditions and Acceptable Usage Policy before you even think about doing so and putting yourself at risk of inconvenience or liability! These are almost always available on the ISP's website, or on demand from the ISP.

As an example, the AUP for BT's (British Telecom) broadband service (that is available at `http://www.abuse-guidance.com/`) says the following about port scanning:

"You must not run "port scanning" software, which accesses remote machines or networks, except with the explicit prior permission of the administrator or owner of such remote machines or networks. This includes using applications capable of scanning the ports of other internet users. [...]

If you intend to run a port scanning application, you must provide BT with a copy of the written consent received from the target of the scan authorizing the activity. This must be supplied to BT prior to the application being run."

This is fairly similar, if a little bureaucratic, to the type of AUP most ISPs issue.

An example scan using the scanner Nmap might look something like this:

```
james@horus: ~ $ sudo nmap 10.10.2.32 -T Insane -O

Starting nmap 3.81 ( http://www.insecure.org/nmap/ ) at 2006-05-02
21:36 BST
Interesting ports on 10.10.2.32:
(The 1662 ports scanned but not shown below are in state: closed)
PORT    STATE SERVICE
22/tcp open  ssh
MAC Address: 00:30:AB:19:23:A9 (Delta Networks)
Device type: general purpose
Running: Linux 2.4.X|2.5.X|2.6.X
OS details: Linux 2.4.18 - 2.6.7
Uptime 0.034 days (since Tue May  2 20:47:15 2006)

Nmap finished: 1 IP address (1 host up) scanned in 8.364 seconds
```

As we can see in this scan, there is one port from the default set of 1663 ports that Nmap version 3.81 scans that is open—port 22, or the port that SSH runs on. Since this is an unfirewalled Linux host, Nmap can also detect uptime for the system (using TCP Timestamping, RFC1323, http://www.faqs.org/rfcs/rfc1323.html). We can also guess when the machine was last rebooted, and based on idiosyncrasies pertaining to the way in which the machine has responded to a variety of non-standard packets sent to it by Nmap during the scanning process, Nmap performs an **OS Fingerprint** (requested through the use of the -O flag) on the host, with fairly good accuracy.

Nmap is an extremely powerful tool, and one of the most commonly used IT security tools on the planet. The (newly rewritten) manual page (man Nmap, or from the website — http://www.insecure.org/nmap/man/) is not only very informative as to how the tool is to be used, but also as to how it works and why.

Other scanners that you might want to try, particularly on a Windows platform (in which Nmap is somewhat fiddly to install and is frequently prevented from working by service packs and patches) include Superscan (http://www.foundstone.com/index.htm?subnav=resources/navigation.htm&subcontent=/resources/proddesc/superscan.htm).

Looking at a default configuration of the IPCop firewall from the internal network (i.e. if you port scan your server from the Green zone, or if an employee, child, or client connected to a corporate network were to scan the firewall), port 445 is the only port we will see open.

Many port scanners (including Nmap), however, do not scan every port to which it is possible to connect on a server as we can see from the preceding scan—Nmap scans 1663 *commonly used* ports by default. This is done for two reasons: firstly, the less data we send (and receive), the quicker the scan; secondly, the more data we send and receive, the more likely the scan is to arise suspicion (or cause network problems)—hopefully not a concern for the legitimate user of a tool such as Nmap!

Since it is common to scan only well-known ports, therefore, we have a practical example of one piece of hardening that has already been carried out—a change in port from 443 to 445 (which is not a common services port). This may be "security through obscurity" but it is *not a bad thing*—apart from making any connections that are made to this port a lot more obvious (they must necessarily come from a deliberate connection attempt rather than accidental browsing or an automated worm affecting HTTP servers via HTTPS), it genuinely will reduce the effectiveness of (subtle) network reconnaissance on the part of an intruder.

Port scanning, then, enables us to establish *which services are running on our firewall* from the internal network.

What about externally? Well, port scanning is just as valuable here too (if not more so).

Port scanning externally allows us to test whether the ports that the Internet sees as open on the external interface of our firewall correspond with any port forwards or holes that we have opened outside our firewall. For the same reasons as port scanning hosts internally, this is an important port of a proactive security policy.

Although we can check which ports we are allowing into our network via the IPCop GUI, port scanning is another way in which we can verify that our port forwards are forwarding to the appropriate place. Ports that we have forwarded to hosts inside the network, and which do not show up on a port scan (which are filtered), may also be identified in this manner; although we can view which ports are forwarded in the web interface, we cannot verify that there is anything to which the ports are being forwarded. In a large environment in which we are not aware of all of the forwarded ports, this may be one way of identifying unneeded holes (which we can remove) in our firewall.

Some websites, such as Sygate's, (`http://scan.sygatetech.com/`) will port scan your host for you automatically (for free) and present you with the results via the Web. This is useful if your ISP is restrictive or you don't have another computer directly connected to the Internet to scan from!

What is Running on Our Firewall?

In addition to auditing our firewall to see what ports it is listening on, we may also routinely audit it in order to identify which processes are running on the firewall. There are several packages that can aid us with this.

At the simplest, binutils such as the `ps` command, which lists processes running on a system, may be used to ascertain what our system is doing. The `top` command, which displays processes in real time and can be used to watch processes on a system (such as to monitor unpredictable processes and find out what is causing poor performance) may also be used here.

The `ps` command, however, is not ideal for these situations. The prime reason for this is: it is very easy for an intruder to replace the `ps` command with a version that does not display malicious processes (a collection of tools performing tasks such as this for an intruder is commonly referred to as a **rootkit**). Another reason for this is that it is fairly time consuming to compare `ps` output, and this requires relatively detailed knowledge of processes on a system (and many malicious processes may be disguised as legitimate processes even if the `ps` output has not been directly altered).

There are, luckily for us, many other applications we can use to prevent, and detect, scenarios in which our system has been tampered with. The first of these, and one of the older tools used on Unix and Linux systems, is called tripwire (`http://sourceforge.net/projects/tripwire`). Tripwire is a Host Intrusion Detection System (HIDS), an application that will monitor specific files on a system (such as system binaries like `ps`, and configuration files). Tripwire does not monitor in real time, but rather seeks to detect such changes after the act. Tripwire can alert us to these events both for security purposes and others (such as change management or simply part of the normal IT Process).

Tripwire is an open-source tool, and is available as an addon for IPCop.

Another useful tool for these scenarios is chkrootkit (`http://www.chkrootkit.org/`). Like tripwire, chkrootkit inspects files on the system, but chkrootkit is a script initiated at user request to scan specifically for files recognized as malicious. Although useful to run periodically for verification processes, the old adage that prevention is better than cure holds true, and a negative scan by no means indicates that a system is clear. As chkrootkit is a script, you can download the script using the `wget` command, or upload it to your server using `scp` (`http://www-hep2.fzu.cz/computing/adm/scp.html`) at a command prompt, and run the freshly downloaded copy straight on the server.

SCP

SCP, or Secure CoPy, is a subset of the functionality included with the SSH server/client that are included with IPCop. Using the `scp` command at a Unix/Linux command prompt, or a tool such as WinSCP (`http://winscp.sourceforge.net`) on Windows, you can access the filing system on your IPCop system and manipulate the filing system remotely. Although extremely useful, `scp` is easy to manipulate for nefarious purposes, and as such, shell access should be carefully guarded and protected.

Advanced Hardening

By this point, we are aware of two large changes we can make to our operations and setup of IPCop, to make it more secure. The first, auditing open ports, allows us to cut down the exposure that our firewalls and systems have to the Internet. The second, utilizing some form of intrusion detection or after-the-fact scanning system such as tripwire and chkrootkit, gives us a higher chance of detecting anyone who does happen to break through our defenses.

Hardening our host, however, is a lot more comprehensive a task than simply installing a service or running some port scanning software. Maintaining a hardened system involves removing any functionality that we don't need as well as making well thought-out changes to our system's security. IPCop is already considerably hardened in this respect, making it considerably securer than a default Linux installation of any of the major distributions. Some of the steps that have been made to make IPCop more secure include the following.

Stack-Smashing Protector (Propolice)

Stack-Smashing Protector (SSP) (`http://www.research.ibm.com/trl/projects/security/ssp/`) is a patchset for the GCC Compiler, used to create the binary executable files that constitute software in IPCop and many other open-source applications, developed by Hiroaki Etoh of IBM. SSP helps to protect exploits in computer software that manipulate the *stack*, an area to which data is added and removed, such as buffer overrun attacks.

In a **buffer overrun** attack, an attacker may exploit a bug in a piece of software to write data to areas of memory that are adjacent to an area of memory assigned to that data (such as a heap or a stack). When this situation exists, a malicious application may be written in order to allow an attacker to run his or her own (malicious) code on a system, generally compromising security.

SSP protects against attacks on the stack by verifying that the stack is not altered, and causing any application in which this occurs to **segmentation fault**, and exit. All software on IPCop, which is compiled with this feature, therefore, is afforded some protection against certain sorts of attack commonly used to exploit systems.

Service Hardening

IPCop has unnecessary services removed by default—many operating systems, including widely deployed versions of Linux and older versions of the Windows operating systems, run many services that are unnecessary to normal operations. Common examples of these include web servers such as IIS server on Windows and the Apache server on Windows or Linux, or processes such as finger, nfs, portmap, telnet, etc., which are not used in the majority of deployments.

As each one of these processes carries a risk of an exploit such as a buffer overflow being used to break into the system, each service that is eliminated closes another door for a potential intrusion. An intrusion may vary from a worm such as the Code Red worm (which exploited a buffer overflow in the IIS web server) in 2001 or Slapper worm (which exploited a buffer overflow in the OpenSSL handshake process to compromise the Apache web server) in 2002, all of the way through to a more precise attack by a malicious intruder.

If we do not need services such as SSH or Squid that are included with IPCop, or services installed via addons, then, best practice is not to enable them, and preferably to remove them from the system entirely. Although services like SSH and Apache, which are commonly exposed to the Internet, carry less risk than services less commonly exposed, such as Squid, any service not required should as a matter of course be removed.

Logfiles and Monitoring Usage

As part of good security management, it is important to retain the capacity to notice trends in behavior and usage of information systems, which allow us to notice changes proactively. A change in usage of a proxy server, memory usage, or CPU load may indicate something innocuous, such as a rise in user activity or a need for upgraded hardware, a hardware fault, or even malicious activity.

Establishing a Baseline with Graphs

It is important, therefore, to establish a *baseline* for how our server behaves in order to be able to identify when a particular piece of behavior is out of the ordinary. IPCop aids us greatly here by providing us with graphical tools to monitor (and graph) statistics such as proxy connections and CPU usage. It is important for the security of your host that you regularly review these and account for any major blips or alterations in behavior.

The authors have been aware of several situations in which systems have been compromised and used for malicious purposes, and in which traffic monitoring on routers upstream from the systems have indicated a rise in traffic. The resulting investigation has subsequently uncovered the malicious activity, and resulted in the servers being shut down and cleansed.

Logfiles

Logfiles are another important part of security management and another frequent indication of malicious activity. It is important for administrators to read through their logfiles and, again, establish a baseline for events produced by their server. Logfiles such as the Apache web server logs and the /var/log/auth.log file, which stores authentication events, are very significant and often provide invaluable information about attempts to break into a system, guess passwords, or gather information on a system. This might include attempts to use brute force to discover usernames and passwords via an SSH server or an HTTP server such as the IPCop management interface.

Auditing SSH Log Events

As a result of malicious worms online, crude brute force attempts to log into SSH servers on the default port of 22 are a very common part of life online. Virtually any SSH server connected to the Internet will most likely have large numbers of log events generated with common system accounts such as root and admin being unsuccessfully logged into. These are relatively normal, and make a compelling argument for moving SSH to an alternative port (as IPCop does by default) in order to be able to distinguish between attempts like these and genuine break in attempts.

An example of logs from /var/log/auth.log caused by a brute force attempt on an SSH server might look like this:

```
Apr 30 09:34:48 firewall sshd[28936]: Illegal user library from
217.160.209.42
Apr 30 09:34:48 firewall sshd[28938]: Illegal user test from
217.160.209.42
Apr 30 09:34:50 firewall sshd[28944]: Illegal user admin from
217.160.209.42
```

```
Apr 30 09:34:50 firewall sshd[28946]: Illegal user guest from
217.160.209.42
Apr 30 09:34:50 firewall sshd[28948]: Illegal user master from
217.160.209.42
Apr 30 09:34:53 firewall sshd[28960]: Illegal user admin from
217.160.209.42
Apr 30 09:34:53 firewall sshd[28962]: Illegal user admin from
217.160.209.42
Apr 30 09:34:53 firewall sshd[28964]: Illegal user admin from
217.160.209.42
Apr 30 09:34:54 firewall sshd[28966]: Illegal user admin from
217.160.209.42
Apr 30 09:34:55 firewall sshd[28972]: Illegal user test from
217.160.209.42
Apr 30 09:34:55 firewall sshd[28974]: Illegal user test from
217.160.209.42
Apr 30 09:34:56 firewall sshd[28976]: Illegal user webmaster from
217.160.209.42
Apr 30 09:34:56 firewall sshd[28978]: Illegal user username from
217.160.209.42
Apr 30 09:34:56 firewall sshd[28980]: Illegal user user from
217.160.209.42
Apr 30 09:34:57 firewall sshd[28984]: Illegal user admin from
217.160.209.42
Apr 30 09:34:58 firewall sshd[28986]: Illegal user test from
217.160.209.42
Apr 30 09:34:59 firewall sshd[28994]: Illegal user danny from
217.160.209.42
Apr 30 09:35:00 firewall sshd[28996]: Illegal user alex from
217.160.209.42
Apr 30 09:35:00 firewall sshd[28998]: Illegal user brett from
217.160.209.42
Apr 30 09:35:00 firewall sshd[29000]: Illegal user mike from
217.160.209.42
```

Logfiles are generally relatively self-explanatory, and in cases where this is not true, documentation for the packages in question (such as OpenVPN (http://www. openvpn.net), OpenSSH (http://www.openssh.com), and the Apache web server (http://www.apache.org)) is often extremely good.

Usage and Denial of Service

Not all security risks stem from the compromise of software and credentials. Many security risks commonly referred to as **Denial of Service**, or **DoS**, attacks, affect the quality of service offered by a computer system, and can be just as damaging as a system compromise. If your firewall is down and you cannot send email to a customer to confirm a business deal, the loss of revenue could be greater than if your firewall were compromised and the intruder knew about the deal.

It is extremely important for the security of our systems to ensure that the hardware they run on is adequate, and therefore performance monitoring, as mentioned during Chapter 5, should be carried out regularly, and unusual activity, such as high network or CPU usage, should be accounted for. Such administration forms an important part of making sure that our firewall is not only secured against simple attacks, but is also resilient both against DoS attacks and surges in usage.

If one performance counter (or several) appears to be unusually high or has recently spiked, there are several things we can do to troubleshoot the problem. It is possible, particularly if our hardware is of lower specification (a Pentium II or less) and our network is relatively fast (five Mbit or faster) that the machine is simply under load — use of the IDS (Snort) or proxy server (Squid) will increase the load on the processor and increase memory usage.

CPU and Memory Usage

The first thing we can look at if CPU usage is high is which application is using the CPU! Although there isn't much useful diagnostic information for this via the web GUI, we can fortunately use the `top` utility to view which processes are running on our system, along with statistics such as the percentage of memory and CPU time that they are using.

```
10.1.2.20 - PuTTY                                              _ □ ✕

top - 10:24:13 up 5 min,  2 users,  load average: 0.00, 0.02, 0.00
Tasks:   27 total,   1 running,  26 sleeping,   0 stopped,   0 zombie
Cpu(s):   0.4% user,   0.0% system,   0.0% nice,  99.6% idle
Mem:     62516k total,    21896k used,    40620k free,     2900k buffers
Swap:   124924k total,       0k used,   124924k free,    11788k cached

  PID USER      PR  NI  VIRT  RES  SHR S %CPU %MEM    TIME+  COMMAND
  390 root      18   0  1028 1028  844 R  0.4  1.6  0:00.17 top
    1 root       8   0   568  568  500 S  0.0  0.9  0:05.12 init
    2 root       9   0     0    0    0 S  0.0  0.0  0:00.00 keventd
    3 root      19  19     0    0    0 S  0.0  0.0  0:00.00 ksoftirqd_CPU0
    4 root       9   0     0    0    0 S  0.0  0.0  0:00.00 kswapd
    5 root       9   0     0    0    0 S  0.0  0.0  0:00.00 bdflush
    6 root       9   0     0    0    0 S  0.0  0.0  0:00.00 kupdated
   14 root       9   0     0    0    0 S  0.0  0.0  0:00.01 kjournald
   36 root       9   0     0    0    0 S  0.0  0.0  0:00.00 kapmd
   47 root       9   0     0    0    0 S  0.0  0.0  0:00.00 kjournald
   48 root       9   0     0    0    0 S  0.0  0.0  0:00.02 kjournald
   88 root       9   0   628  628  540 S  0.0  1.0  0:00.01 syslogd
   90 klogd      9   0  1196 1196  576 S  0.0  1.9  0:00.10 klogd
  268 dnsmasq    9   0   712  712  616 S  0.0  1.1  0:00.00 dnsmasq
  295 root       9   0   680  680  592 S  0.0  1.1  0:00.00 fcron
  306 root       9   0  2312 2312 2120 S  0.0  3.7  0:00.00 httpd
  311 nobody     8   0  2668 2668 2280 S  0.0  4.3  0:00.00 httpd
  312 nobody     8   0  2720 2720 2312 S  0.0  4.4  0:00.05 httpd
  316 root       9   0  1524 1524 1312 S  0.0  2.4  0:00.00 sshd
  327 root       8   0  1576 1576 1280 S  0.0  2.5  0:00.06 bash
  328 root       9   0   488  488  424 S  0.0  0.8  0:00.00 mingetty
  329 root       9   0   488  488  424 S  0.0  0.8  0:00.00 mingetty
  330 root       9   0   488  488  424 S  0.0  0.8  0:00.01 mingetty
  331 root       9   0   488  488  424 S  0.0  0.8  0:00.01 mingetty
  332 root       9   0   488  488  424 S  0.0  0.8  0:00.00 mingetty
  375 root      11   0  1760 1760 1500 S  0.0  2.8  0:00.06 sshd
  378 root      10   0  1560 1560 1276 S  0.0  2.5  0:00.03 bash
```

Although it may look a little intimidating, the output from the `top` command is fairly logical, and updates dynamically as you are looking at it. The `top` output above is from a clean IPCop 1.4.10 system (with no proxy server or IDS configured), and most of the processes listed are self-explanatory.

Processes beginning with the letter `k` are all (in this example) kernel processes. `sshd`, unsurprisingly, is the SSH server process (the `d` stands for **Daemon**, which in Unix and Linux terminology essentially means server process). The `httpd` is what provides us with the HTTP-based GUI; `dnsmasq` is both a DNS and DHCP server. `syslogd` keeps system logs, and `mingetty` and `bash` are all processes that handle and provide the text-based console.

In this instance, there is very little CPU usage — **99.6%** **idle**, and **0.4%** of actual usage is thanks to top alone! We can take it, then, that there are no performance-related problems with this system (or that they're so pervasive that top itself is affected and giving phony output — this would be highly unlikely unless the system had been compromised and top itself replaced by an attacker).

In the following example, we can see that there is **29.7%** CPU usage — there is a second root logon (a new bash and sshd process will appear for each user logged on via SSH), responsible for running the grep command (which looks for a specific piece of text in a file, or large number of files), which is using a lot of CPU time (and probably a lot of disk time as well). This is a second logon for the purpose of this example, and the grep command being run (which will consume CPU time and use the disk, but shouldn't break anything) was grep -r * foo, run from the root of the filing system (cd / at a command line).

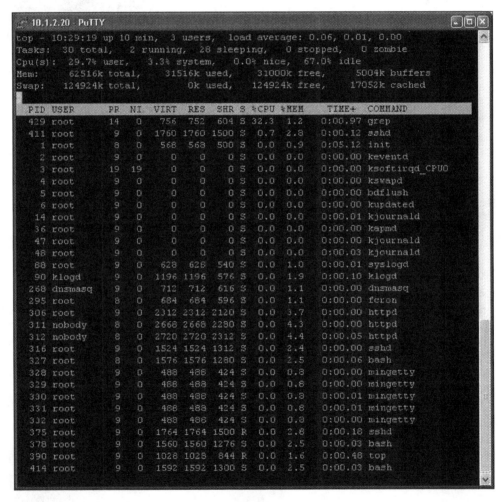

It is a good idea to know which processes are running on your system. Although many intrusions will involve replacements of binary files such as those that run ps and top, it is often the case that a break in that does not have root (administrator) access to the system will have processes running that are visible via ps or top. Invisible processes, or modified versions of binary files such as ps and top, may be detected by applications such as chkrootkit.

If your Squid proxy, HTTP server, or another process was heavily using CPU or memory, you might have an issue with it (or potentially, an attacker) requiring attention. We can also use the ps command to list processes running on the system, although the ps command included in IPCop is part of the busybox toolkit, which is less powerful than the *real* (binutils version) ps included with most Linux systems.

Logged-In Users

We can view users logged in via SSH using the w command as shown in the following figure:

As we can see, there are three instances of the root user logged in: the first, on tty1, is logged into the physical terminal on the IPCop host itself, while the pts/0 and pts/1 terminals are both virtual terminals, accessed via SSH. The **WHAT** column indicates which process the user is currently interactively running — in the second session, w (w will detect itself running while enumerating processes running on the system), while both other sessions are at bash, which is the name of the command line itself (i.e. the other two users are either idle, or typing at the command line without having a specific application in the foreground).

Mastery of administration of a Linux system is complex, but there are several simple tools that IPCop comes with, such as top, ps, w, netstat, and route, which can show us (respectively) live and snapshotted process information, logged-in users, network connections, and the routing table. Knowledge of these and some basic understanding of networking and the architecture of the Linux operating system will get us a long way in diagnosing problems, analyzing intrusions, and resolving performance issues.

Other Security Analysis Tools

There are many other tools besides those that we have mentioned that help us to analyse the state of our firewall and look for security holes. Many smaller utilities such as Nmap have a very specific purpose, while some tools are broader in scope. Nessus, a security scanner, is worthy of particular attention due to the scope of usage that it has. Nessus collates a number of different security holes together, and has the ability to look for these holes on one host, or across an entire network.

Some of the holes that Nessus will report may be false positives, and Nessus may be unsure in these cases whether a particular, insecure, configuration is present. Alternatively, the false positive may be an enabled feature that *should* be disabled, but is instead in use. Either way, Nessus, while useful, is a tool that is worth using with care, particularly on a system such as IPCop, which is carefully engineered not to be maintained in quite a normal way.

Nevertheless, on your IPCop system as well as other systems (such as servers, workstations, printers, switches, and wireless access points), Nessus is capable of picking up a wide variety of security holes and common misconfigurations. Read more about Nessus at http://www.nessus.org/.

Where to Go Next?

It can seem like you're living in a vacuum, unable to get assistance with issues like security, and without enough information to further your understanding of the topics. Luckily, this is not the case, and there are many resources online with large amounts of information on topics pertaining to security. Some of the good examples have been mentioned here.

Full-Disclosure

If there were ever a center for the online security community, you could make a very compelling case that it was Full-Disclosure.

Started in response to other, moderated, mailing lists in which information was not freely available and censorship was a routine part of online discussions about security, the concept of Full-Disclosure promotes the complete availability of information, and as the name of the list implies, the mailing list promotes these ideals.

In accordance with these principles, then, the list is completely unmoderated (apart from rare instances of highly antisocial behavior such as spamming or repeated and distasteful offensiveness) and promotes full availability of information about security. Full-Disclosure is a busy list populated by people from all walks of the security community. More information is available from the Full-Disclosure charter at http://lists.grok.org.uk/full-disclosure-charter.html.

Wikipedia

Although Wikipedia is not generally thought of as a security-specific information source, many of the articles on technical topics such as TCP/IP, firewalls, and computer security are extremely good, and the computer security article makes a great starting place, as it has links to Wikipedia articles and third-party resources that are extremely comprehensive (see http://en.wikipedia.org/wiki/Computer_security).

SecurityFocus

Although not vendor-neutral (SecurityFocus is owned by AntiVirus vendor Symantec), SecurityFocus is a good portal site with many good articles written by knowledgeable contributors. SecurityFocus is also the home of many good mailing lists, including the well-known Bugtraq (see http://www.securityfocus.com).

Literature

There are many good books about security, on a wide range of topics. Some of these are very broad and go out of date very quickly, while some cover extremely detailed topics. A very random selection of (relatively) well-regarded books on different topics is:

Counter Hack Reloaded: A Step-by-Step Guide to Computer Attacks and Effective Defenses, ISBN 0-13-148104-5

This highly acclaimed book from Ed Skoudis and Tom Liston represents a fairly comprehensive overview of computer security, starting out with networking, covering operating system security in both Unix and Windows environments, network reconnaissance, software flaws, and a variety of attacks and hacking techniques. This is a good, serious, approachably technical introduction to security.

The Art of Deception: Controlling the Human Element of Security, ISBN 0-47-123712-4

This less technical book by Kevin Mitnick covers the topic of Social Engineering, the breaking of computer systems by manipulating people. This involves telephone calls, masquerading as a staff member, pretending to be from a utility company, or even bribery, to gain physical and logical access to computer systems and information about them.

Hacking Exposed 5th Edition, ISBN 0-07-226081-5

This relatively technical book in its fifth edition represents a broad view of hacking with relevance to a number of different technologies. Although it has a slightly sensational cover and demeanor, and it will not teach you all you need to know about hacking or computer security overnight, it does cover some of the fundamental topics in security as well as demonstrate, practically, how computers are compromised, and is not a bad starter for someone new to security.

TCP/IP Illustrated 3 Volume Set, ISBN 0-20-177631-6

This classic book by Richard W. Stevens is often touted as *the* book on TCP/IP Networking, and is an excellent (if highly technical, at points) primer on how TCP/IP works. Along with the IBM redbook mentioned in Chapter 7 on networking, this is well worth reading for anyone interested in security, as (particularly with respect to firewalls) the understanding of how networking works is critical to your understanding of security on networked computer systems.

Linux Server Security, Second Edition, ISBN 0-59-600670-5

This relatively technical book is an excellent primer on—as the name implies—Linux server security, from filing system permissions and database security to iptables. It is well worth reading for anyone interested in running Linux servers.

The Tao of Network Security Monitoring: Beyond Intrusion Detection, ISBN 0-32-124677-2

This relatively technical book written by Richard Bejtlich, the founder of a security company, covers not only the flaws of traditional intrusion detection, but also many skills important to a network, security, or firewall administrator, such as the use of `tcpdump` and IDS analysis tools.

Summary

More than anything, the most important skill to master in securing (or just administering) any computer system is the ability to find what information you need when you need it, in as short a space of time as possible. More often than not, this information is available online—if you know where to look—and books like these often prime you with enough knowledge that you can go off and learn about more complex topics yourself. Sites similar to the ones we've mentioned before, such as Wikipedia and SecurityFocus, and mailing lists like Full-Disclosure and the SecurityFocus mailing lists make excellent starting points and sport a very broad selection of users and types of content posted on a daily basis.

Even if you don't become a regular user or poster, it is worth subscribing to Full-Disclosure for a month or two if you're even vaguely serious about security!

We have reviewed some common attitudes towards security, reviewed some of the security measures IPCop provides, and some security measures we can take, both technical and operational, as well as provided some starting points for interested readers to learn more about security.

Computer security is an enjoyable, complex, high profile, and somewhat fashionable topic, making it highly compelling as a source for further study!

11

IPCop Support

We have now covered the topic of IPCop and are aware of its uses within our network and whether IPCop is useful for our particular network and organization. The driving force behind IPCop is its open-source nature and the community behind it, which we have tried to emphasize throughout this book.

We have seen how collections of quite simple tools can create very complex and powerful systems. We also know how to configure these tools using the IPCop interface and how to manage and enhance IPCop itself. This is all possible because of the strong open-source community behind IPCop. Including all user and developers, who constantly further the development of IPCop to create a system that can truly be an effective SOHO router, firewall, and powerful network appliance. As we have shown throughout, the tools involved are numerous and there are many developers and users involved. Combining all the developers of all the tools involved in IPCop easily runs into multiple thousands of highly skilled personnel creating the product we use.

It doesn't stop there however, after all of this work they still offer us more. These same developers who wrote the system, compiled, tested, debugged, and shipped it also offer their time to help support users using it.

Support

There are a number of support mechanisms for IPCop as with most open-source software. The most accessible of these is the IPCop website itself http://www.ipcop.org, which has documentation, tutorials, and FAQs. It helps any open-source project immensely, if users check the IPCop website for any questions that they need answers for, before using the other support mechanisms that might distract another user or developer from their own tasks. If we have problems that this book doesn't address and we can't find the solutions by searching the Web with our favorite search engine or by searching the IPCop website, then we can consider alternative support mechanisms.

User Mailing Lists

There are two mailing lists you should pay particular attention to:

- **Announce**: This mailing list has infrequent announcements relating to IPCop and is usually limited to notification of new releases or important security updates. It can be found at `http://lists.sourceforge.net/mailman/listinfo/ipcop-announce`.

- **Users**: This is a busy discussion list for users of IPCop to seek support from each other and often from the IPCop developers themselves. You should go here with ideas for new features, help with current features, or as a preliminary check when you believe you have found a bug in the IPCop software. This list can be found at `http://lists.sourceforge.net/mailman/listinfo/ipcop-users`.

Internet Relay Chat (IRC)

IRC is the most common location for quick support queries relating to open-source software and Freenode, the network that hosts the #ipcop channel, has a variety of official support channels for open-source software. You will often find around 50 users online at any point in time—the authors being among the regular visitors. Most users in this channel help each other out and hang around discussing the product, comparing it to other products, and very often discussing feature requests or "wish lists".

You may not always get support with addons on the regular support areas. It is often better to go directly to the source, in this case the addon developers, to get comprehensive support on their product.

Returning the Support

Many people feel the need or the obligation to give something back to a project they have found useful and IPCop offers such avenues.

The most obvious way to support open-source software is by furthering the software development. Users are welcome to develop for IPCop and can do so by creating addons as many users have done, or by writing code for the core of IPCop itself, which is often welcomed by the current developers as it eases the load and ensures that IPCop can be developed in all areas that require attention.

There are two development mailing lists for IPCop:

- IPCop-Devel: This is the development mailing list, with discussion on patches that should or shouldn't be included in IPCop, and help for developers working on IPCop. It can be found at `http://lists.sourceforge.net/mailman/listinfo/ipcop-devel`.

- IPCop-CVS: A no chatter, CVS announcement list for notifying developers of any changes to CVS, without them having to log in to the CVS system. This can be found at `http://lists.sourceforge.net/mailman/listinfo/ipcop-cvs`.

You can't donate cash directly to IPCop as this adds the complication of handling charitable donations as a duty for the IPCop developers and requires added, unnecessary, administration. You can, however, elect to pay the developers themselves in order to work on IPCop. This is the simplest way to give money in support of their efforts.

There is no obligation to support the project in anyway but most of us realize that if we like a project and support it, we can generally help it get better or help maintain it. Another example of support is writing books and other documentation, such as this one that brings more users to the project by lowering the skills barrier required and ensuring everything is adequately explained.

Writing code is often seen as the only real way to contribute to an open-source software project but as you can see there are many other options all of which are apparently welcome by the IPCop development team.

Summary

As a user of IPCop, you are allowed to use the software in any way you wish and can even redistribute it, even modified, if needed. The software can be taken in another direction much like IPCop's own creation where it was forked from Smoothwall. This ensures that the software stays around and is useful for years to come, as you can be confident that there will be enough users turned into developers to keep the project going.

You can take the knowledge gained in this book and use it to create the network device that fits your specifications and modify and tune it as necessary. There are options and choices and the software has the protection of the GPL to allow it to survive any issues it has. This means that you can be quite confident in the choice of software as your network doesn't rely on a corporation staying afloat but rather on thousands of users and developers around the world, showing that they can and will work together in order to create truly remarkable software.

Index

DHCP server 93, 94
DNS and default gateway 93
DNS domain name 90
hostname, assigning to IPCop machine 89
installing finished 94
ISDN configuration 90
locale settings 88
network configuration 91
Green network interface, PCop
about 48
addressing on 48
Grub 95

H

host-to-net connections
certificates used 150-153
pre-shared keys used 149, 150
X.509 certificates 150, 151, 154
Host Intrusion Detection System 203
HTTP problem 164
hub
about 15
working 15

I

ICMP 124
ICS
about 67
drawbacks 68
removing 71
IDS. *See* **intrusion detection system**
Internet Connection Sharing. *See* **ICS**
Internet Control Message Protocol 124
intrusion detection system
about 127
benefit 128
categories 127
HIDS 127
introduction 127
need for 128
NIDS 127, 129
promiscuous mode 129
Snort 127, 129
working 129
intrusion prevention system
about 127

IPCop
addons 171
advantages 45, 46
Apache used 44
bandwidth 163
benefits 42, 43
Blue zone 159
building on stable components, benefits 44
certificates with IPSec in IPCop 155, 156
common addons 175
components for topology one, NAT firewall 70
customizing 171
development mailing lists 219
distribution of software 40
DNS server 36
DSL technology 50
features 46
firewall, attaching to DSL line 50
firewall, checking status 109
firewall addons server 171
firewall functionality 121
firewall hardening 198
firewalling rules for topology one, NAT firewall 71
first boot 95, 96
forking 41
forking with SmoothWall 42
for SOHO network 45
for topology one, NAT firewall 69
functionalities for topology one, NAT firewall 70
functionality, altering 67
Green interface configuration 86
hardware considerations 82
hardware requirements 81
ICS 67
installation, hard drive partitioning and formatting 85
installation media 84
installing 83, 84
installing equipment 82, 83
installing finished 94
Intrusion Detection System 71
intrusion detection system 127
intrusion prevention system 127
IPCop box for topology three 76

R

Red network interface
about 49
addressing on 49
analog modem 51
cable and satellite internet 52
DSL technology 49
ISDN modem 51
remote access
about 137
routers
about 19
for client networks 19
illustration 20, 21

S

SCP 204
security
about 195
baseline, establishing with graphs 205
common issues 197
components for securing systems 196
Denial of Service 207
IPCop 198
literature 213, 214
logfiles 206
Nessus, security analysis tool 212
Nmap, security analysis tool 212
online security community 213
open source community 217
security analysis tools 212
SecurityFocus 213
system hardening 196
systems, securing 196
Wikipedia 213
server
about 14
uses 15
services, IPCop
about 56, 115
advanced network services 60
DHCP 57
DHCP server 115, 116
dynamic DNS 57, 117, 118, 119
dynamic DNS, settings 59
dynamic DNS providers 118

dynamic leases 117
edit hosts 120
fixed leases 116, 117
FQDN 58
Network Time Protocol 59
Network Time Server 60
Network Time Server, using 121
NTP 120
port forwarding 61, 62, 119
RED IP 118
time server 120
web proxy 56, 57
SID 131
Simple Network Management Protocol 198
SmoothWall
about 41
SmoothWall and IPcop 41
Snort
about 128
ACID, analysis option 134
as sniffer 128
BASE, analysis option 134
introduction 128
log analysis option 133
logs 130
priority levels 132
setting up with IPCop 130
SnortALog, analysis option 133
SnortALog, features 133
SnortSnarf, analysis option 133
using with IPCop 130
source code 40
Squid
about 165
configuring 165, 166
history 165
SquidGuard
about 176
configuration 176, 178
configuration options 176, 177
configuration screen 176
SSH access
about 100, 101
connecting to SSH 101
SSH, using to tunnel network traffic 104
SSH access page 105
SSH protocols 103

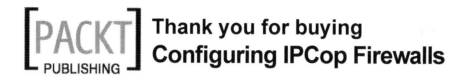

Thank you for buying
Configuring IPCop Firewalls

Packt Open Source Project Royalties

When we sell a book written on an Open Source project, we pay a royalty directly to that project. Therefore by purchasing Configuring IPCop Firewalls, Packt will have given some of the money received to the IPCop project.

In the long term, we see ourselves and you—customers and readers of our books—as part of the Open Source ecosystem, providing sustainable revenue for the projects we publish on. Our aim at Packt is to establish publishing royalties as an essential part of the service and support a business model that sustains Open Source.

If you're working with an Open Source project that you would like us to publish on, and subsequently pay royalties to, please get in touch with us.

Writing for Packt

We welcome all inquiries from people who are interested in authoring. Book proposals should be sent to authors@packtpub.com. If your book idea is still at an early stage and you would like to discuss it first before writing a formal book proposal, contact us; one of our commissioning editors will get in touch with you.

We're not just looking for published authors; if you have strong technical skills but no writing experience, our experienced editors can help you develop a writing career, or simply get some additional reward for your expertise.

About Packt Publishing

Packt, pronounced 'packed', published its first book "Mastering phpMyAdmin for Effective MySQL Management" in April 2004 and subsequently continued to specialize in publishing highly focused books on specific technologies and solutions.

Our books and publications share the experiences of your fellow IT professionals in adapting and customizing today's systems, applications, and frameworks. Our solution-based books give you the knowledge and power to customize the software and technologies you're using to get the job done. Packt books are more specific and less general than the IT books you have seen in the past. Our unique business model allows us to bring you more focused information, giving you more of what you need to know, and less of what you don't.

Packt is a modern, yet unique publishing company, which focuses on producing quality, cutting-edge books for communities of developers, administrators, and newbies alike. For more information, please visit our website: www.PacktPub.com.

OpenVPN: Building and Integrating Virtual Private Networks

ISBN: 1-904811-85-X   Paperback: 258 pages

Learn how to build secure VPNs using this powerful Open Source application

1. Learn how to install, configure, and create tunnels with OpenVPN on Linux, Windows, and MacOSX

2. Use OpenVPN with DHCP, routers, firewall, and HTTP proxy servers

3. Advanced management of security certificates

Openswan: Building and Integrating Virtual Private Networks

ISBN: 1-904811-25-6   Paperback: 350 pages

Learn from the developers of Openswan how to build industry standard, military grade VPNs and connect them with Windows, MacOSX, and other VPN vendors

1. Learn everything you need to know about Openswan from its core developers

2. Build VPNs that interoperate with Windows, MacOS, and other network vendors

3. Build your own secure hotspots

Please check **www.PacktPub.com** for information on our titles

PUBLISHING

Building Responsive Web Applications
AJAX and PHP

AJAX and PHP: Building Responsive Web Applications

ISBN: 1-904811-82-5   Paperback: 275 pages

Enhance the user experience of your PHP website using AJAX with this practical tutorial featuring detailed case studies

1. Build a solid foundation for your next generation of web applications

2. Use better JavaScript code to enable powerful web features

3. Leverage the power of PHP and MySQL to create powerful back-end functionality and make it work in harmony with the smart AJAX client

4. Go through 8 case studies that demonstrate how to implement AJAX-enabled features in your site

Drupal

Creating Blogs, Forums, Portals, and Community Websites
How to setup, configure, and customise this powerful PHP/MySQL-based Open Source CMS

David Mercer

Drupal: Creating Blogs, Forums, Portals, and Community Websites

ISBN: 1-904811-80-9   Paperback: 267 pages

How to setup, configure and customise this powerful PHP/MySQL based Open Source CMS.

1. Install, configure, administer, maintain and extend Drupal

2. Control access with users, roles and permissions

3. Structure your content using Drupal's powerful CMS features

4. Includes coverage of release 4.7

Please check **www.PacktPub.com** for information on our titles

www.ingramcontent.com/pod-product-compliance
Lightning Source LLC
Chambersburg PA
CBHW082117070326
40690CB00049B/3597